Cook's Corner

Skinny Comfort Food

igloobooks

igloobooks

Published in 2018
by Igloo Books Ltd
Cottage Farm
Sywell
NN6 0BJ
www.igloobooks.com

Food photography and recipe development:
© Stockfood, The Food Media Agency
Cover image © iStock / Getty Images
Additional imagery: © iStock / Getty Images

STA002 0618
2 4 6 8 10 9 7 5 3
ISBN: 978-1-78810-189-9

Cover designed by Nicholas Gage
Interiors designed by Simon Parker
Edited by Jasmin Peppiatt

Printed and manufactured in China

Cook's Corner

Skinny Comfort Food

Contents

Cook's Corner

Skinny Comfort Food
Breakfasts

Breakfast waffle sandwich

SERVES: 1 | PREP TIME: **10 MINUTES** | COOKING TIME: **10 MINUTES**

INGREDIENTS

65 g / 2 ¼ oz / ½ cup plain flour

½ tsp baking powder

½ tsp salt

2 eggs

100 ml / 3 ⅓ fl. oz buttermilk

100 g / 3 ½ oz streaky bacon

50 g curly leaf lettuce

1 tomato, sliced

METHOD

1. Mix together the flour, baking powder and salt in a large mixing bowl. Beat one of the eggs and, using a wooden spoon, mix into the dry ingredients with the buttermilk until you have a smooth batter. Leave to stand for 10 minutes while your waffle iron heats up.

2. Pour the batter into the waffle maker and cook until steam stops rising and the mixture is golden brown.

3. While the waffle is cooking, cut all fat off the bacon then place it under a medium hot grill and cook for 10 minutes, turning once, until crisp.

4. Cut the waffle in half and add the lettuce and tomato, then top with the cooked bacon. Heat a little oil in a pan and fry the remaining egg adding to the sandwich.

5. Season and top off the sandwich with the remaining half of the waffle.

Fruity breakfast granola

SERVES: 1 | PREP TIME: 10 MINUTES

INGREDIENTS

300 ml / 10 fl. oz 0% fat yogurt

100 g / 3 ½ oz / ⅔ cup mixed frozen black forest berries, defrosted

100 g / 3 ½ oz / ⅔ cup fresh strawberries

30 g / 1 oz / ⅓ cup granola

METHOD

1. Place half of the yogurt into a blender and mix with the black forest berries. Blend until smooth and set aside.

2. Blend the other half of the yogurt with 80 grammes of the strawberries until smooth.

3. Chop the remaining strawberries and place most of them into the bottom of a serving cup. Top with some of the granola and then the strawberry yogurt.

4. Add another layer of granola before topping with the black forest berry yogurt. Finally top with the remaining granola and remaining strawberries.

5. Garnish with further berries and mint leaves, if desired.

Waffles

SERVES: 4 | PREP TIME: 10 MINUTES | COOKING TIME: 25 MINUTES

INGREDIENTS

250 g / 9 oz / 1 ⅔ cups plain (all-purpose) flour

2 tsp baking powder

2 large eggs

300 ml / 10 ½ fl. oz / 1 ¼ cups milk

2 tbsp melted low-fat butter

sunflower oil, for oiling the waffle maker

icing (confectioner's) sugar to serve

METHOD

1. Put the oven on a low setting and put an electric waffle maker on to heat.

2. Mix the flour and baking powder in a bowl and make a well in the centre.

3. Break in the eggs and pour in the milk then use a whisk to gradually incorporate all of the flour from around the outside, followed by the melted butter.

4. Spoon some of the batter into the waffle maker and close the lid.

5. Cook for 4 minutes or according to the manufacturer's instructions until golden brown.

6. Repeat until all the batter has been used, keeping the finished batches warm in the oven.

7. Dust the waffles with a little icing sugar before serving, if more sweetness is desired.

Chocolate and banana granola

SERVES: 6 | PREP TIME: 5 MINUTES | COOKING TIME: 5 MINUTES

INGREDIENTS

200 ml / 7 fl. oz / ¾ cup light cream

200 g / 7 oz dark chocolate
(min. 70% cocoa solids), chopped

4 bananas, sliced

4 tbsp granola

METHOD

1. Heat the cream until it starts to simmer, then pour it over the chopped chocolate and stir until the mixture has cooled and thickened.

2. Layer the chocolate ganache with the sliced banana inside six glasses and top with a sprinkle of granola.

Muffins with scrambled egg

SERVES: 4 | PREP TIME: 10 MINUTES | COOKING TIME: 5 MINUTES

INGREDIENTS

8 large eggs

2 tbsp low-fat butter

4 English breakfast muffins, halved and toasted

chopped basil leaves, to garnish

METHOD

1. Gently beat the eggs, with a pinch of salt and pepper, to break up the yolks.

2. Heat the butter in a non-stick frying pan until sizzling then pour in the eggs.

3. Cook over a low heat, stirring constantly until the eggs scramble.

4. Divide the mixture between the halved muffins.

5. Garnish with the chopped basil leaves and serve immediately.

Smoked salmon bagels

SERVES: 4 | PREP TIME: 5 MINUTES | COOKING TIME: 4 MINUTES

INGREDIENTS

4 sesame bagels

125 g / 4 ½ oz / ½ cup low-fat cream cheese

2 tbsp fresh dill, finely chopped

½ lemon, juiced

½ cucumber, thinly sliced

8 slices smoked salmon

METHOD

1. Heat a griddle pan until smoking hot. Slice the bagels in half and toast them on the griddle for 2 minutes on each side or until nicely marked.

2. Mix the cream cheese with the dill and lemon juice and season to taste.

3. Spread the bottom half of the bagels with the cream cheese mixture and arrange the cucumber slices and salmon on top.

4. Position the other half of the bagels on top and serve while the bread is still a little warm from the griddle.

Egg, avocado and rye bread

SERVES: 1 | PREP TIME: 10 MINUTES

INGREDIENTS

1 ripe avocado

2 slices German style rye bread, toasted

½ tsp chilli (chili) flakes

½ lemon, juice only

1 tbsp olive oil

2 eggs

a handful of fresh parsley, finely chopped

METHOD

1. Peel and de-stone the avocado before cutting into slices. Place on top of the toast before sprinkling over the chilli flakes and a squeeze of lemon juice.

2. Heat the oil in a frying pan over a medium hot heat. Add the eggs and fry for 3-4 minutes until cooked. Remove from the pan with a spatula and place on top of the avocado before seasoning and garnishing with the chopped parsley.

Pancakes

SERVES: 4 | PREP TIME: 10 MINUTES | COOKING TIME: 30 MINUTES

INGREDIENTS

250 g / 9 oz / 1 ⅔ cups plain (all-purpose) flour

2 tsp baking powder

2 large eggs

300 ml / 10 ½ fl. oz / 1 ¼ cups
skimmed milk

2 tbsp melted low-fat butter

butter, to serve

METHOD

1. Mix the flour and baking powder in a bowl and make a well in the centre. Break in the eggs and pour in the milk. Whisk all of the flour in from round the outside.

2. Melt the low-fat butter in a frying pan then whisk into the batter. Put the pan back over a low heat. You will need a tablespoon of batter for each pancake and you should be able to cook 4 pancakes at a time.

3. Spoon the batter into the pan and cook for 2 minutes. Turn the pancakes over with a spatula and cook the other side.

4. Repeat until all the batter has been used.

5. Pile the pancakes onto warm plates and top each one with a knob of low-fat butter.

Blueberry and kiwi chia pudding

SERVES: 4 | PREP TIME: 15 MINUTES | COOKING TIME: 10-14 MINUTES

INGREDIENTS

500 ml / 17 fl. oz / 2 cups low-fat coconut milk

3 tsp of coconut nectar

½ cup chia seeds

1 tsp vanilla extract

150 g / 5 ¼ oz / 1 cup blueberries

200 ml / 7 fl. oz / ¾ cup zero fat natural yogurt

1 kiwi fruit, peeled and sliced

METHOD

1. Combine the coconut milk, coconut nectar, chia seeds and vanilla extract in a bowl.

2. Place the blueberries into a blender and blend for 1-2 minutes until smooth. Pass through a sieve to remove the skins, pressing down with the back of a spoon to get all the juice.

3. Mix the blueberry juice into the chia mixture before covering. Refrigerate for at least four hours or overnight so that the seeds have absorbed the liquid and expanded.

4. Fold the natural yogurt into the chia pudding to loosen before spooning into serving glasses. Top the pudding with the slices of kiwi before serving.

Fresh berry porridge

SERVES: 1 | PREP TIME: 5 MINUTES | COOKING TIME: 12-15 MINUTES

INGREDIENTS

50 g / 1 ¾ oz / ½ cup whole porridge oats

200 ml / 7 fl. oz / ¾ cup skimmed milk

1 tsp fruit syrup

50 g / 1 ¾ oz / ½ cup mixed berries

1 tbsp pomegranate seeds

METHOD

1. Place the oats into a saucepan with the milk and place onto a medium heat.

2. Cook the oats with the milk stirring continuously for 12-15 minutes until the oats have softened and the milk has been absorbed. Add more milk if you prefer your porridge less thick.

3. Stir through the fruit syrup to sweeten to your own taste.

4. Spoon into a serving bowl and top with the fruit and pomegranate seeds.

Baked eggs with tomato

SERVES: 2 | PREP TIME: 10 MINUTES | COOKING TIME: 15 MINUTES

INGREDIENTS

2 large tomatoes

125 g / 4 ¼ oz lighter mozzarella

a handful of basil leaves, chopped

2 tbsp olive oil

2 large free-range eggs

METHOD

1. Preheat the oven to 180°C (160°C fan) / 350F / gas 4.

2. Slice the tomatoes and mozzarella into roughly equal sized rounds and place into a bowl.

3. Add half the basil and the oil to the bowl and toss the ingredients together, seasoning with salt and black pepper.

4. Place alternate layers of mozzarella and tomato into two ramekins. Carefully break an egg into the top of each before placing onto a baking tray and transferring to the oven.

5. Cook for 12-15 minutes until the egg is set, remove and season again before scattering with the remaining basil.

Salmon scrambled eggs

SERVES: 4 | PREP TIME: 2 MINUTES | COOKING TIME: 5 MINUTES

INGREDIENTS

8 large eggs

3 tsp low-fat butter

3 slices smoked salmon, chopped

chives, chopped

METHOD

1. Gently beat the eggs with a pinch of salt and pepper to break up the yolks.

2. Heat the butter in a frying pan until sizzling then pour in the eggs.

3. Cook over a low-medium heat, stirring until the eggs start to scramble.

4. Stir in the salmon and chopped chives and cook for 1 more minute or until done to your liking.

5. Place the scrambled egg and salmon onto a toasted bagel or muffin and top with more chives, if desired.

Dairy-free rice pudding

SERVES: 2 | PREP TIME: 10 MINUTES | COOKING TIME: 20 MINUTES

●●●●●●●●●●●●●●●●●●●●●●●●●●

INGREDIENTS

1 tbsp dairy-free spread

85 g / 3 oz / ½ cup pudding rice

250 ml / 8 ½ fl. oz almond milk

1 tsp vanilla paste

2 tbsp agave syrup

2 tsp cinnamon

2 tsp nutmeg

METHOD

1. Melt the dairy-free spread in a large heavy
    bottomed saucepan before adding the rice,
    milk, vanilla and half the agave syrup. Stir
    the mixture together and reduce to a very
    low heat. Cook gently for 30 minutes or until
    the rice is tender and the mixture has
    thickened and become creamy.

2. Spoon into serving bowls before topping
    with the remaining agave syrup, cinnamon
    and nutmeg.

Skinny Comfort Food

Lunches and main meals

Sausage, leek and potato casserole

SERVES: 4-6 | PREP TIME: 25 MINUTES | COOKING TIME: 30 MINUTES

INGREDIENTS

200 g / 7 oz potatoes, peeled

6 reduced fat pork sausages

1 onion, diced

3 leeks, sliced

2 carrots, diced

2 garlic cloves, finely chopped

500 ml / 17 fl. oz reduced salt chicken stock

150 ml / 5 fl. oz light single cream

1 bay leaf

100 g / 3 ½ oz / ½ cup reduced fat cheese, grated

spring onion (scallion), chopped

METHOD

1. Preheat the oven to 180 C. Bring a pan of salted water to the boil and add the potatoes. Cook for 10 minutes so that they are parboiled, drain and set aside.

2. In a large oven-proof casserole cook the sausages for about 15 minutes, until browned, and remove. Add the onion, leek and carrots and fry them off in the fat from the sausages, adding a little oil if necessary. Cook for 10 minutes until softened, then add the garlic and cook for a further minute. Chop the sausages into large pieces and return them to the pan.

3. Add the stock to the pan and bring to the boil and then reduce to a simmer. Add the cream and bay leaf and cook for 5 minutes, seasoning to taste.

4. Slice the potatoes and place them on top of the casserole in layers, before topping with the grated cheese. Place in the oven and cook for 30 minutes, it will be ready once the potatoes are tender. Garnish with the chopped spring onion.

Baked chicken with raw salad

SERVES: 2 | PREP TIME: 20 MINUTES | COOKING TIME: 25 MINUTES

INGREDIENTS

1 tbsp olive oil

1 tsp cumin seeds

1 tsp fennel seeds

1 tsp dried oregano

4 chicken drumsticks, or thighs

1 courgette (zucchini), halved lengthways and finely sliced

400 g / 14 oz cooked chickpeas, drained

½ red onion, finely sliced

200 g / 7 oz sweetcorn, drained

1 tbsp red wine vinegar

4 tbsp extra virgin olive oil

1 lemon, juiced

a small bunch of fresh parsley, chopped

1 little gem lettuce

a handful of cherry tomatoes

METHOD

1. Preheat the oven to 200°C (180°C fan) / 400F / gas 6. In a bowl combine the oil, cumin seeds, fennel seeds and oregano and seasoning. Add the chicken to the bowl and mix around in the marinade to coat the chicken. Place into an oven-proof dish and bake in the oven for 20-25 minutes until golden.

2. While the chicken is cooking, add the courgette, chickpeas, red onion and sweet corn to a bowl. In a small jar with a lid, mix together the vinegar, oil and lemon and shake well to combine. Season with salt and pepper to taste. Pour this mixture over the mixed vegetables, adding the parsley, and toss to coat.

3. In a serving bowl, arrange the lettuce leaves and top with the vegetables, cooked chicken and tomatoes. Drizzle with a little oil and season to taste.

Tomato and thyme soup

SERVES: 4 | PREP TIME: 5 MINUTES | COOKING TIME: 30 MINUTES

INGREDIENTS

2 tbsp olive oil

1 onion, finely chopped

4 cloves of garlic, crushed

2 tbsp thyme leaves

450 g / 1 lb ripe tomatoes, diced

500 ml / 17 ½ fl. oz / 2 cups vegetable stock

METHOD

1. Heat the oil in a saucepan and fry the onion for 8 minutes or until softened.

2. Add the garlic and half of the thyme to the pan and cook for 2 more minutes, then stir in the tomatoes and vegetable stock and bring to the boil.

3. Simmer for 20 minutes then blend until smooth with a liquidizer or immersion blender.

4. Taste the soup and adjust the seasoning with salt and pepper, then ladle into bowls and sprinkle with the rest of the thyme.

Goulash

SERVES: 2-4 | PREP TIME: 15 MINUTES | COOKING TIME: 1 HOUR, 30 MINUTES

INGREDIENTS

500 g / 1 lb 1 oz lean stewing beef, cubed

low calorie cooking spray

1 tbsp low-fat butter spread

1 onion, diced

1 tsp sweet paprika

1 tsp ground marjoram

1 tsp ground caraway seeds

1 tbsp tomato purée

2 carrots, sliced

300 ml / 10 ½ fl. oz / 1 ¼ cups reduced salt beef stock

METHOD

1. Wash the meat and pat dry.

2. Spray a casserole pan with the oil and warm to a medium high heat. Sear the meat in the pan before removing and setting aside.

3. Add the butter spread to the pan and turn down the heat to medium. Add the onion to the pan and cook for 4-5 minutes until softened. Stir the spices and tomato purée into the onions and cook for a minute.

4. Return the beef to the pan with the carrots and stock. Cover and leave to cook for up to 90 minutes. Season to taste before serving.

Moussaka

SERVES: 8 | PREP TIME: 20 MINUTES | COOKING TIME: 45 MINUTES

INGREDIENTS

180 ml / 6 fl. oz cup olive oil

2 large aubergine (eggplant), sliced

1 onion, diced

3 garlic cloves, finely chopped

500 g / 1 lb lean lamb mince

400 g / 14 oz tin of chopped tomatoes

1 tsp sage, chopped

1 tsp rosemary, chopped

500 ml / 17 fl. oz low-fat yogurt

2 eggs, beaten

1 tsp grated nutmeg

1 lemon, juice and zest

50 g / 1 ¾ oz / ½ cup low-fat feta cheese, crumbled

100 g / 3 ½ oz cherry tomatoes, halved

50 g / 1 ¾ oz / ½ cup Parmesan cheese, grated

METHOD

1. Heat half the oil in a large heavy bottomed frying pan over a medium high heat. Coat the sliced aubergine in flour and fry on each side until golden brown. Place on kitchen paper to drain.

2. Preheat the oven to 190°C (170°C fan) / 375F / gas 5. Add the remaining oil to the pan and fry the onion for 5 minutes until golden brown. Add the garlic and cook for a further minute before adding the lamb mince. Fry for 10 minutes until browned then add the tomatoes. Bring to the boil then simmer for 20 minutes and add the chopped herbs.

3. In a bowl, mix together the yogurt, egg, nutmeg, lemon and feta cheese, season and set aside.

4. In an ovenproof dish, add a layer of lamb before topping with a layer of aubergine, repeat this again before topping with the yogurt mix. Add the remaining aubergine and chopped tomatoes before sprinkling with the cheese. Bake for 30 minutes or until the top is golden brown and the yogurt mixture has set.

Bacon and egg scones

MAKES: 12 | PREP TIME: 25 MINUTES | COOKING TIME: 12-15 MINUTES

INGREDIENTS

225 g / 8 oz / 1 ½ cups self-raising flour

55 g / 2 oz / ¼ cup low-fat butter

150 ml / 5 fl. oz / ⅔ cup skimmed milk

FOR THE FILLING

4 large eggs

4 rashers streaky bacon

4 tbsp light mayonnaise

cress to garnish

METHOD

1. Preheat the oven to 220°C (200° fan) / 425F / gas 7 and oil a large baking sheet.

2. Sieve the flour into a bowl and rub in the butter until the mixture resembles fine breadcrumbs. Stir in enough milk to bring the mixture together into a soft dough.

3. Flatten the dough with your hands on a floured work surface until 2.5 cm (1 inch) thick.

4. Use a pastry cutter to cut out 12 circles and transfer them to the baking sheet.

5. Bake in the oven for 10–15 minutes or until golden brown and cooked through. Transfer the scones to a wire rack to cool a little while you make the filling.

6. Boil the eggs for 6 minutes then drain and plunge into cold water for 4 minutes.

7. Meanwhile, grill the bacon for 3 minutes on each side or until crisp, then roughly chop. Peel the eggs and mash them with a fork then mix with the bacon pieces and mayonnaise.

8. Split open the scones and fill with the bacon and egg mayonnaise and a sprinkle of cress.

Thai green curry

SERVES: 2 | PREP TIME: 20 MINUTES | COOKING TIME: 20 MINUTES

INGREDIENTS

250 g / 9 oz / 1 ¼ cups Thai jasmine rice

1 tsp groundnut oil

2 tbsp Thai green curry paste

1 aubergine, diced

4 kaffir lime leaves

1 stick lemongrass, bruised

1 tbsp fish sauce

1 can low-fat coconut milk

500 g / 1 lb turkey breast, cut into strips

small bunch of coriander (cilantro),
stalks and leaves

1 fresh green chilli (chili) sliced

1 lime

METHOD

1. In a saucepan, cook the rice as per the packet instructions and keep warm whilst you prepare the curry.

2. In a large wok, heat the oil over a medium high heat. Add the curry paste and fry for 2 minutes until fragrant. Add the aubergine, lime leaves, lemongrass and fish sauce, continuing to fry for a further 2 minutes. If the ingredients are looking a little dry add a splash of the coconut milk.

3. Pour in the coconut milk before adding the turkey. Bring to the boil and then reduce to a simmer for 12-15 minutes, adding the chopped coriander stalks, until the meat is cooked. Serve in a bowl and garnish with the chopped coriander leaves, chilli and a lime wedge.

Cream cheese and salad rolls

SERVES: 4 | PREP TIME: 5 MINUTES

INGREDIENTS

4 oat-topped wholemeal rolls, halved

125 g / 4 ½ oz / ½ cup cream cheese

1 medium tomato, sliced

½ cucumber, sliced

4 lettuce leaves

METHOD

1. Spread the bottom half of the rolls thickly with cream cheese and arrange the tomato, cucumber and lettuce on top.

2. Sandwich with the other half of the rolls and serve immediately.

Vegetable soup

SERVES: 4 | PREP TIME: 5 MINUTES | COOKING TIME: 20 MINUTES

INGREDIENTS

2 tbsp olive oil

2 leeks, sliced

2 cloves of garlic, crushed

4 spring onions, chopped

2 courgettes, chopped

1 red pepper, sliced

1 orange pepper, chopped

150 g / 5 ½ oz / 1 cup broad beans, defrosted if frozen

1 litre / 1 pint 15 fl. oz / 4 cups vegetable stock

flat leaf parsley, to serve

METHOD

1. Heat the oil in a saucepan and fry the leeks for 5 minutes or until softened.

2. Add the garlic and vegetables to the pan and cook for 2 more minutes, then stir in the vegetable stock and bring to the boil.

3. Simmer for 10 minutes then season to taste with salt and pepper.

4. Ladle the soup into 4 warm bowls and garnish with parsley.

Sausage and onion gravy

SERVES: 4 | PREP TIME: 5 MINUTES | COOKING TIME: 30 MINUTES

INGREDIENTS

8 reduced fat sausages

2 red onions, cut into wedges

2 tbsp runny honey

1 tbsp Dijon mustard

250 ml / 9 fl. oz / 1 cup chicken stock

METHOD

1. Preheat the oven to 180°C (160° fan) / 350F / gas 4.

2. Arrange the sausages and onion wedges in a baking dish and season with salt and pepper.

3. Mix the honey with the mustard then slowly incorporate the chicken stock.

4. Pour the mixture over the sausages and onions then transfer the dish to the oven.

5. Bake for 30 minutes, turning the sausages and stirring the onions half way through.

Chicken korma

SERVES: 4 | PREP TIME: 30 MINUTES | COOKING TIME: 45 MINUTES

INGREDIENTS

450 g / 1 lb skinless chicken breast, cubed

2 tbsp korma curry powder

2 tbsp olive oil

1 onion, finely chopped

1 red chilli (chili), finely chopped

2 cloves of garlic, crushed

200 g / 7 oz / 1 cup canned tomatoes, chopped

400 ml / 14 fl. oz / 1 ⅔ cups coconut milk

4 tbsp ground almonds

2 tbsp mango chutney

METHOD

1. Mix the chicken with the curry powder and leave to marinate for 30 minutes.

2. Heat the oil in a large saucepan and fry the onion and chilli for 3 minutes. Add the garlic and cook for 2 minutes.

3. Add the chicken and cook for 4 minutes, stirring occasionally, until it starts to colour on the outside.

4. Add the chopped tomatoes, coconut milk, ground almonds and mango chutney and bring to a gentle simmer.

5. Cook the curry for 35 minutes, stirring occasionally, until the chicken is tender and the sauce has thickened.

Toad in the hole

SERVES: 4 | PREP TIME: 10 MINUTES | COOKING TIME: 50 MINUTES

INGREDIENTS

1 tbsp olive oil

6 venison sausages

150 g / 4 oz / 1 cup plain flour

¼ tsp salt

1 egg

300 ml / 10 fl. oz / 1 ¼ cups skimmed milk

METHOD

1. Heat a medium-sized baking dish in the oven with the oil to 220°C (200°C fan) / 425F / gas 7. After 2 minutes, add the sausages and cook for 10-15 minutes, turning occasionally, until browned.

2. Meanwhile, mix the flour and salt in a medium sized mixing bowl. Using a wooden spoon, beat in the egg and enough milk to form a stiff, smooth batter. Set aside for 5 minutes and then gradually beat in the remaining milk. Cover and set aside.

3. Remove the sausages from the oven and, while still hot, pour the batter into the dish. Return to the oven and reduce to 180°C / 350F / gas 4 and bake for 30 minutes until the batter has risen and turned golden brown.

41

Chicken and black bean stew

SERVES: 4 | PREP TIME: 20 MINUTES | COOKING TIME: 40 MINUTES

INGREDIENTS

1 tbsp olive oil

4 chicken thighs, skinless and boneless

100 g / 3 ½ oz chorizo, sliced

1 onion, diced

2 garlic cloves, finely chopped

2 red peppers, roughly chopped

400 g / 14 oz chopped tomatoes

200 ml / 7 fl. oz water

400 g / 14 oz tinned black beans, drained

parsley, chopped

METHOD

1. Heat the oil over a medium heat in a large heavy bottomed pan. Roughly chop the chicken and brown in the hot oil, remove with a slotted spoon and set aside.

2. Add the sliced chorizo to the pan and fry for 2-3 minutes until the oil has turned golden yellow. Remove from the pan and set aside with the chicken.

3. Add the onion to the pan and cook for 2-3 minutes until translucent, add a little more oil if needed. Add the garlic and fry for a further minute before adding the peppers. Cook for a further 2-3 minutes before adding the chopped tomatoes and water. Return the chicken and chorizo to the pan and bring to the boil before turning down to a simmer. Cover and cook for 20 minutes, adding the beans for the final 5 minutes.

4. Season with salt and black pepper to taste and serve in the pan with the chopped parsley scattered on the surface.

Sardine and egg panini

SERVES: 4 | PREP TIME: 5 MINUTES | COOKING TIME: 3 MINUTES

INGREDIENTS

120 g / 4 oz canned sardines in oil

2 large ciabatta rolls, halved

2 boiled eggs, sliced

rocket (arugula) to serve

METHOD

1. Put an electric panini press on to heat.

2. Mash the sardines into their oil with a fork and spread them over the bottom halves of the rolls.

3. Top with the boiled egg slices, season with salt and pepper, then sandwich together with the top of the rolls.

4. Toast the panini for 3 minutes or according to the manufacturer's instructions.

5. Cut the panini into four pieces each and serve two pieces per person with some rocket on the side.

Macaroni cheese

SERVES: 4 | PREP TIME: 10 MINUTES | COOKING TIME: 30 MINUTES

INGREDIENTS

350 g / 12 oz macaroni pasta

2 tbsp low-fat butter

1 garlic clove, finely chopped

1 tsp English mustard

3 tbsp plain flour

500 ml / 17 fl. oz skimmed milk

350 g / 12 oz / 3 ½ cups low-fat mature Cheddar, grated

METHOD

1. Cook the pasta as per instructions so that it is slightly al dente. Drain well and set aside.

2. In a saucepan, melt the butter and add the garlic. Fry for 1 minute before stirring in the mustard and flour. Cook for a further minute before gradually adding the milk, whisking constantly. Once all the milk has been added, continue to cook the thickened sauce for 5 minutes. Remove from the heat and stir in 250 grammes of the cheese and season.

3. Preheat the oven to 200°C (180°C fan) / 400F / gas 6. Combine the pasta with the sauce before pouring into an oven proof dish. Sprinkle over the remaining grated cheese and bake in the oven for 20 minutes.

Paella with chorizo

SERVES: 4 | PREP TIME: 20 MINUTES | COOKING TIME: 30 MINUTES

INGREDIENTS

1 tbsp olive oil

100 g / 3 ½ oz chorizo, sliced

1 onion, diced

1 red pepper, diced

2 garlic cloves, minced

1 tsp paprika

250 g / 9 oz / 1 ¼ cups paella rice

500 ml / 17 fl. oz reduced salt chicken stock

1 tsp saffron

200 g / 7 oz mixed seafood, cooked

100 g / 3.5 oz octopus, tinned

150 g / 5 oz peas, cooked and drained

1 lemon, juiced

1 bunch flat leaf parsley, finely chopped

METHOD

1. In a wide pan, heat the olive oil over a medium heat and fry the chorizo for 2 minutes until browned. Remove with a slotted spoon and set aside.

2. Add the onion and fry for 3 minutes before adding the peppers and cooking for a further 2 minutes. Add the garlic and paprika and fry for a further minute. Stir the rice into the pan and pour in the stock and add the saffron, bring to the boil and then reduce and simmer for 15-20 minutes, stirring occasionally, until the stock has been absorbed and the rice is cooked.

3. Return the chorizo to the pan and add the seafood, octopus and peas and gently heat. Before serving, add the lemon juice, stir through the parsley and season.

4. Serve with lemon wedges.

Mini fish pies

SERVES: 6 | PREP TIME: 10 MINUTES | COOKING TIME: 30-35 MINUTES

INGREDIENTS

450 g / 1 lb potatoes, peeled and cubed

500 ml / 17 ½ fl. oz / 2 cups milk

1 bay leaf

400 g / 14 oz smoked haddock fillet

4 tbsp low-fat butter

2 tbsp plain flour

METHOD

1. Preheat the oven to 200°C (180° fan) / 400F / gas 6.

2. Cook the potatoes in boiling salted water for 12 minutes or until tender then drain well. Meanwhile, put the milk and bay leaf in a small saucepan and bring to a simmer.

3. Lay the haddock in a snugly-fitting dish and pour the hot milk over the top. Cover the dish with cling film and leave to stand for 10 minutes.

4. Heat half of the butter in a small saucepan and stir in the flour.

5. Reserve 2 tablespoons of the haddock milk for the potatoes and strain the rest into the butter and flour mixture, stirring constantly. Cook until the sauce is thick and smooth.

6. Remove any skin and bones from the haddock then flake the flesh into the white sauce. Season to taste with salt and black pepper then divide the mixture between 6 individual pie dishes.

7. Mash the potatoes with the reserved milk and remaining butter and spoon it on top of the haddock. Bake the pies for 15 minutes or until the topping is golden brown.

49

Pad Thai noodles

SERVES: 2 | PREP TIME: 10 MINUTES | COOKING TIME: 10 MINUTES

INGREDIENTS

200 g / 7 oz raw king prawns

small bunch of coriander, stalks finely chopped

½ red onion, sliced

1 tsp chilli (chili) flakes

2 packs of straight to wok pad thai noodles

100 g / 3 ½ oz beansprouts

1 egg, beaten

1 lime, juiced

1 tbsp fish sauce

3 spring onions (scallions), sliced

1 tbsp roasted peanuts, chopped

METHOD

1. Heat a wok to a high heat and add the prawns and coriander stalks and fry until the prawns turn pink, roughly 3 minutes. Add the red onion and chilli flakes and fry for a further minute keeping everything in the pan moving.

2. Add the noodles, beansprouts, egg, lime and fish sauce and continue to cook for a further 2-3 minutes until the egg is cooked and the noodles have been heated through.

3. Divide between two serving bowls and top with the chopped coriander leaves, spring onions and chopped peanuts and serve with lime wedges.

Slow-cooked shredded beef

SERVES: 4-6 | PREP TIME: 15 MINUTES | COOKING TIME: 6 HOURS

INGREDIENTS

1 kg / 2 lb 3 oz extra lean beef joint

1 tsp smoked paprika

1 tsp dried oregano

1 tsp garlic granules

1 tsp cumin

300 ml / 10 ½ fl. oz / 1 ¼ cups reduced salt beef stock

2 bay leaves

METHOD

1. Preheat the oven to 140°C (120°C fan) / 275F / gas 1.

2. Rub the beef all over with the paprika, oregano, garlic and cumin before seasoning with salt and black pepper.

3. Place the beef into a roasting tray and pour in the beef stock before adding the bay leaves. Tightly seal the tray with a double layer of foil.

4. Place the meat into the oven and roast for 5-6 hours. Remove from the oven and shred the meat into the cooking juices. Season to taste before serving.

51

Buttermilk biscuits and gravy

SERVES: 4 | PREP TIME: 15 MINUTES | COOKING TIME: 30 MINUTES

INGREDIENTS

30 g / 1 oz / ⅓ cup butter

170 g / 6 oz / 1 ¼ cups flour

1 tsp salt

1 tsp baking powder

½ tsp bicarbonate of soda

150 ml / 5 fl. oz buttermilk

1 tbsp rapeseed oil

500 g / 1 lb lean pork mince

½ onion, finely chopped

3 tbsp plain flour

450 ml / 15 fl. oz skimmed milk

METHOD

1. Preheat the oven to 220°C (200°C fan) / 425F / gas 7, lightly grease a baking tray.

2. In a mixing bowl, mix the flour, salt, baking powder and bicarbonate. Using your fingertips rub in the butter until rough breadcrumbs form. Stir in the buttermilk until a soft dough forms.

3. Knead on a floured surface for 1 minute, roll out to around 2 cm thickness. Using a 2-inch pastry cutter, cut out and place onto the baking tray. Bake in the oven for 15 minutes until a skewer inserted into the centre of a scones comes out clean.

4. While the biscuits are baking, heat the oil in a large frying pan and add the pork mince and onion. Fry for 10 minutes until browned before adding the flour and stirring through for 2 minutes. Gradually add the milk mixing it in completely after each addition until you have a thick gravy.

5. Season and add tabasco, if desired.

6. Halve the freshly baked biscuits and top with the hot gravy.

Lamb stuffed peppers

SERVES: 4 | PREP TIME: 15 MINUTES | COOKING TIME: 45 MINUTES

INGREDIENTS

1 tbsp olive oil

1 onion, diced

2 garlic cloves, crushed

500 g / 1 lb lean lamb mince, 10% fat

1 tsp dried oregano

1 tsp dried basil

200 g / 7 oz / 1 cup pearl barley

400 g / 14 oz chopped tomatoes

250 ml / 8 ½ fl. oz water

4 large red peppers

50 g / 1 ¾ oz / ½ cup feta cheese

mint, chopped

METHOD

1. Heat the oil in a large heavy based pan over a medium high heat. Add the onions and fry until slightly golden and translucent. Add the garlic and fry for a further minute before adding the mince. Fry the lamb mince for 5 minutes until browned and add the dried herbs.

2. Add the pearl barley to the lamb mince and mix through before adding the chopped tomatoes and water. Bring to the boil and then lower to a simmer and cook for 45 minutes or until the barley is softened.

3. Preheat the oven to 180°C (160°C fan) / 350F / gas 4. Cut the top off the peppers and carefully scoop out the seeds and pith. Fill each of the peppers with the lamb mixture and place them into an ovenproof dish. Crumble over the feta and mint before replacing the tops of the peppers.

4. Bake into the oven for 30 minutes or until the peppers are charred and soft when a knife is inserted and serve immediately.

Roast beef toasted sandwich

SERVES: 4 | PREP TIME: 5 MINUTES | COOKING TIME: 3 MINUTES

INGREDIENTS

8 slices white bread

4 tbsp light mayonnaise

1 tsp Dijon mustard

1 tsp wholegrain mustard

8 slices rare roast beef

4 tbsp French tarragon leaves

METHOD

1. Toast the bread in a toaster or under a hot grill.

2. Mix the mayonnaise with the mustards and season with a little black pepper.

3. Spread the mustard mayonnaise over the toast and top four of the slices with the beef.

4. Scatter over the tarragon leaves, then sandwich with the rest of the toast and cut in half on the diagonal.

Crab cakes

SERVES: 16 | PREP TIME: 20 MINUTES | COOKING TIME: 4-5 MINUTES

INGREDIENTS

4 tbsp plain (all-purpose) flour

1 egg, beaten

75 g / 2 ½ oz / ½ cup panko breadcrumbs

450 g / 1 lb / 2 cups leftover mashed potato

200 g / 7 oz / 1 ¼ cup fresh crab meat

2 spring onions, finely chopped

2 tbsp fresh dill, finely chopped

sunflower oil for deep-frying

METHOD

1. Put the flour, egg and panko breadcrumbs in 3 separate bowls.

2. Mix the mashed potato with the crab, spring onions and dill then shape it into 16 small patties.

3. Dip the crab cakes alternately in the flour, egg and breadcrumbs and shake off any excess.

4. Heat the oil in a deep fat fryer, according to the manufacturer's instructions, to a temperature of 180°C.

5. Lower the crab cakes in the fryer basket and cook for 4 minutes or until crisp and golden brown.

6. Tip the crab cakes into a kitchen paper lined bowl to remove any excess oil.

Sweet potato cottage pie

SERVES: 4 | PREP TIME: 20 MINUTES | COOKING TIME: 1 HOUR, 30 MINUTES

INGREDIENTS

2 tbsp olive oil

1 small onion, finely chopped

2 cloves of garlic, crushed

450 g / 1 lb / 2 cups minced beef

400 g / 14 oz / 1 ¾ cups canned tomatoes, chopped

400 ml / 14 fl. oz / 1 ⅔ cups beef stock

FOR THE TOPPING

2 large sweet potatoes

50 g / 1 ¾ oz / ¼ cup butter

2 tsp fresh thyme leaves

METHOD

1. Preheat the oven to 200°C (180° fan) / 400F / gas 6.

2. Bake the sweet potatoes in their skins for 45 or until a skewer inserted slides in easily.

3. Meanwhile, heat the oil in a large saucepan and fry the onion for 3 minutes, stirring occasionally.

4. Add the garlic and cook for 2 minutes, then add the mince.

5. Fry the mince until it starts to brown then add the chopped tomatoes and stock and bring to a gentle simmer.

6. Cook for 1 hour, stirring occasionally, until the mince is tender and the sauce has thickened a little.

7. When the sweet potatoes are ready, peel off and discard the skins and mash the flesh with the butter and thyme leaves.

8. Spoon the mince mixture into a large baking dish then top with the mashed sweet potatoes.

9. Use a fork to level the surface and make stripes in the potato then bake in the oven for 20 minutes or until golden brown.

Sausage and bean casserole

SERVES: 4 | PREP TIME: 10 MINUTES | COOKING TIME: 45 MINUTES

INGREDIENTS

1 tbsp olive oil

6 low-fat pork sausages

2 rashers back bacon, chopped

1 onion, diced

1 celery stick, finely sliced

2 garlic cloves, chopped

250 g / 9 oz butter beans, soaked overnight

500 ml / 17 fl. oz chicken stock

2 sprigs thyme

2 bay leaves

fresh parsley, chopped

METHOD

1. In a large casserole dish, heat the oil over a medium heat. Add the sausages to the pan and fry for 12-15 minutes until browned. Remove and set aside. Add the bacon to the pan and fry for 3 minutes before adding the onion and celery. Continue to fry for a further 5 minutes until translucent, before adding the garlic and frying for 1 minute.

2. Meanwhile, drain the beans and place into a pan of rapidly boiling salted water for 10 minutes before draining and rinsing.

3. Slice the sausages and return to the casserole with the drained beans. Pour in the chicken stock and add the thyme and bay leaves. Bring to the boil and reduce heat to a simmer for 15 minutes, or until the beans are cooked.

4. Season and top with the chopped parsley before serving.

Chicken fajitas

SERVES: 4 | PREP TIME: 35 MINUTES | COOKING TIME: 8 MINUTES

INGREDIENTS

450 g / 1 lb chicken breast, sliced

2 tbsp fajita seasoning mix

2 tbsp sunflower oil

1 onion, sliced

1 red pepper, sliced

1 yellow pepper, sliced

1 green pepper, sliced

8 soft flour tortillas

guacamole to serve

METHOD

1. Toss the chicken with the seasoning mix and leave to marinate for 30 minutes.

2. Heat the oil in a large frying pan and stir-fry the chicken for 4 minutes.

3. Add the onions and peppers and stir fry for a further 4 minutes, then divide the mixture between the tortillas.

4. Roll up the fajitas and serve with guacamole for dipping.

Seafood salad sandwich

SERVES: 1 | PREP TIME: 10 MINUTES

INGREDIENTS

100 g / 3 ½ oz white and brown crab meat

50 g / 1 ¾ oz king prawn, cooked and chopped

2 tbsp low-fat mayonnaise

1 tsp ketchup

pinch of cayenne

½ lemon, juiced

1 spring onion (scallion), sliced

2 slices wholemeal bread

2 reduced fat cheese slices

METHOD

1. In a bowl, combine the crab, prawn, mayonnaise, ketchup, cayenne, lemon juice and onion. Mix together until well mixed and season with salt and black pepper to taste.

2. Toast the bread and then top with a cheese slice on each. Add the seafood mixture to one of the halves of the sandwich and top with the other.

Couscous and vegetable gratin

SERVES: 6 | PREP TIME: 30 MINUTES | COOKING TIME: 50 MINUTES

300 g / 10 ½ oz / 1 ¾ cups couscous

2 tbsp olive oil

1 carrot, diced

100 g / 3 ½ oz green (string) beans, chopped

100 g / 3 ½ oz / ⅔ cup podded baby broad beans

2 tbsp pine nuts

2 tbsp flat leaf parsley, finely chopped

FOR THE TOPPING

450 g / 1 lb carrots, peeled and chopped

450 g / 1 lb broccoli, broken into florets

100 g / 3 ½ oz / ½ cup butter

50 g / 1 ¾ oz / ½ cup Emmental, grated

1. Preheat the oven to 200°C (180° fan) / 400F / gas 6. To make the topping, cook the carrots and broccoli in separate pans of salted water for 10 minutes, or until they are tender, then drain well. Add half of the butter to each pan, then blend each one to a puree with an immersion blender.

2. Pour 300 ml of boiling water over the couscous then cover and leave to steam for 5 minutes. Meanwhile, heat the oil in a frying pan and fry the vegetables and pine nuts for 5 minutes.

3. Fluff up the couscous grains with a fork and stir in the vegetables and parsley and transfer the mixture to a baking dish. Spread the broccoli puree on top, followed by the carrot puree, then sprinkle with cheese. Bake the gratin for 30 minutes or until golden brown.

Hot dog pizza

MAKES: 1 | PREP TIME: 30 MINUTES | COOKING TIME: 15 MINUTES

INGREDIENTS

100 g / 3 ½ oz / ⅔ cup strong white flour

100 g / 3 ½ oz / ⅔ cup strong wholewheat flour

1 tsp easy-blend dried yeast

125ml / 4 fl. oz warm water

200ml / 6 ½ fl. oz passata

1 tsp dried oregano

150 g / 5 oz light mozzarella cheese

1 shallot, finely sliced

a handful of cherry tomatoes, halved

1 red chilli (chili), sliced

2 chicken or vegetarian hot dogs, sliced

sprig of basil

chilli (chili) oil to drizzle

METHOD

1. Combine the flours, yeast and a pinch of salt in a bowl. Pour in the water and knead for 5 minutes. Roll out on a floured surface and place onto an oiled baking tray.

2. With a ladle, spoon the passata onto the dough and spread evenly, leaving a little space at the edges. Tear the cheese into pieces and scatter over the pizza. Place the tomatoes, shallot, chilli and hot dogs over the pizza and drizzle with a little oil. Leave to rise for 20 minutes. Meanwhile, preheat the oven to 240°C (220°C fan) / 475F / gas 9.

3. Once risen, place into the oven and cook for 12-15 minutes until the base is crisp and cheese has started to brown in places.

4. Scatter with chopped basil and serve.

Chicken burrito bowl

SERVES: 2 | PREP TIME: 15 MINUTES | COOKING TIME: 20 MINUTES

INGREDIENTS

1 tsp ground cumin

1 tsp ground coriander

1 tsp paprika

1 tsp chilli powder

½ tsp salt

1 tbsp olive oil

2 lemons, juiced

2 large organic chicken breast

2 little gem lettuce, roughly chopped

100 g / 3 ½ oz / ½ cup long grain rice, cooked and drained

200 g / 7 oz black beans, cooked and drained

200 g / 7 oz sweetcorn, drained

2 large tomatoes, chopped

1 red onion, diced

fresh coriander (cilantro), chopped

METHOD

1. In a large bowl, combine all the dried spices and salt with the oil and half the lemon juice to create a marinade. Trim the chicken breasts before adding to the marinade and coating. Cover and place in the refrigerator for at least an hour.

2. Preheat the oven to 180°C (160°C fan) / 350F / gas 4. Remove the chicken from the refrigerator at least 20 minutes before cooking.

3. Place on a non-stick baking tray and cook in the oven for around 20 minutes, or until the juices run clear at the thickest part of the meat when pierced with a knife.

4. In a large serving bowl, arrange the lettuce leaves before topping with the rice, which has had the beans mixed through it. Top with the sliced chicken breast. Combine the remaining ingredients in a bowl with the remaining lemon juice and season to taste. Scatter around and over the chicken and serve.

Ravioli with nettle pesto

SERVES: 4 | PREP TIME: 5 MINUTES | COOKING TIME: 5 MINUTES

INGREDIENTS

450 g / 1 lb fresh ravioli

30 g / 1 oz / 2 cups stinging nettles

1 clove of garlic, crushed

1 lemon, zest finely grated

4 tbsp olive oil

100 g / 3 ½ oz ricotta salata, crumbled

METHOD

1. Cook the ravioli in boiling salted water according to the packet instructions or until al dente.

2. Meanwhile, blanch the nettles in boiling water for 10 seconds then drain well and squeeze out all the liquid.

3. Put them in a blender with the garlic, lemon zest and oil and add a good pinch of salt and pepper, then blend to a smooth sauce.

4. Drain the ravioli and split between 4 warm bowls. Spoon over the nettle pesto and top with the ricotta salata.

Mushroom sandwich

SERVES: 1 | PREP TIME: 10 MINUTES | COOKING TIME: 15 MINUTES

INGREDIENTS

1 tbsp coconut oil

½ onion, sliced

50 g / 1 ¾ oz chestnut mushrooms, sliced

1 garlic clove, minced

50 g / 1 ¾ oz red kale, stem removed and roughly chopped

1 tbsp low-fat crème fraiche

2 slices wholemeal bread, toasted

METHOD

1. Heat the oil in a large frying pan on a high heat, add the sliced onion and fry for 5 minutes only stirring very rarely. Once the onion has browned and started to turn golden, add the mushroom. Fry for a further 5 minutes until the mushrooms have started to go crispy at the edges.

2. Turn the heat down to a medium high and add the garlic and kale. Cook for a further 2-3 minutes until fragrant and the kale has softened. Stir in the crème fraiche and season with salt and pepper. Place between the toasted bread and serve.

Vegetable pilaf

SERVES: 4 | PREP TIME: 20 MINUTES | COOKING TIME: 30 MINUTES

INGREDIENTS

3 tbsp oil

1 cinnamon stick

4 cardamom pods

4 cloves

1 onion, sliced

1 tsp turmeric

1 large carrot, cut into batons

1 courgette sliced

250 g / 9 oz mushrooms, sliced

250 g / 9 oz / 1 ¼ cups basmati rice,
washed and soaked

600 ml / 20 fl. oz low salt vegetable stock

400 g / 14 oz can of chickpeas, drained

METHOD

1. Heat the oil in a large heavy based saucepan.
   Fry the cinnamon, cardamom and cloves for
   a few seconds until fragrant. Add the onion
   and cook until golden and translucent.

2. Add the turmeric and fry for a few seconds
   before adding the vegetables. Fry for 5
   minutes, stirring regularly. Add the drained
   rice and fry for a further 5 minutes.

3. Pour the stock into the pan and bring to the
   boil. Reduce the heat and simmer,
   uncovered, for 10 minutes until most of the
   liquid has been absorbed and the rice
   is tender. Add the chickpeas to the pan and
   warm through for a further 4-5 minutes. Mix
   through the rice and check that all the liquid
   has been absorbed.

Roast chicken with lemon

SERVES: 4 | PREP TIME: 15 MINUTES | COOKING TIME: 30 MINUTES

INGREDIENTS

1 tbsp olive oil

4 large chicken thighs

sea salt

2 shallots, sliced

1 preserved lemon, sliced

1 large piece of ginger, peeled and sliced into batons

a handful of black olives

coriander (cilantro), roughly chopped

1 lemon, juiced

METHOD

1. Preheat the oven to 200°C (180°C fan) / 400F / gas 6. In a cast iron skillet, heat the oil over a high heat. Season the skin of the chicken and place skin side down in the pan. Cook for 2 minutes before lowering the heat to medium high and continuing to cook the chicken skin side down for 10 minutes so that the skin is golden brown.

2. Turn the chicken over and add the shallots, lemon, ginger and olives to the pan. Cook for a further 2 minutes. Add 50 ml of water to the pan before transferring to the oven and roasting for 12-15 minutes until the juices of the meat run clear. Remove from the oven and sprinkle over the coriander and lemon juice before serving.

Baked beans and sausages

SERVES: 4 | PREP TIME: 10 MINUTES | COOKING TIME: 4 HOURS, 30 MINUTES

INGREDIENTS

400 g / 14 oz / 2 ⅔ cups dried haricot beans,
soaked overnight

1 large ham hock

400 g / 14 oz / 2 ⅔ cups canned tomatoes, chopped

2 tbsp vegetable oil

8 pork sausages

flat leaf parsley, finely chopped

METHOD

1. Preheat the oven to 150°C (130° fan) / 300F / gas 2.

2. Drain the beans and put them in a large cast iron casserole dish with the ham hock and tomatoes, then add enough cold water to cover it all by 5 cm (2 in)

3. Bring the pan to the boil, then cover and transfer to the oven for 4 hours, topping up with water if it gets too dry.

4. Heat the oil in a frying pan and brown the sausage all over. Stir the baked beans and taste for seasoning, then add the sausages and return to the oven for 30 minutes. Slice the ham off the bone and divide between four warm bowls with the sausages and beans, then sprinkle with parsley.

Sausages and champ potatoes

SERVES: 4 | PREP TIME: 5 MINUTES | COOKING TIME: 20 MINUTES

INGREDIENTS

1 tbsp olive oil

8 low-fat sausages

900 g / 2 lb potatoes, peeled and cubed

250 ml / 9 fl. oz / 1 cup skimmed milk

50 g low-fat butter, cubed

4 spring onions (scallions), roughly chopped

METHOD

1. Heat the olive oil in a frying pan.

2. Fry the sausages for 20 minutes, turning every 3-4 minutes to ensure they cook evenly. Meanwhile, cook the potatoes in boiling water for 10-12 minutes, until tender and starting to break up.

3. Tip the potatoes into a sieve and leave to drain. Return the saucepan to the heat then add the milk and butter. Heat for just a couple of minutes until the milk starts to simmer then take off the heat and return the potatoes to the saucepan.

4. Mash the potatoes in the saucepan until they are smooth. Stir the spring onions into the mashed potato and serve immediately.

Chilli cheese nachos

SERVES: 4-6 | PREP TIME: 5-10 MINUTES |

COOKING TIME: 1 HOUR, 15 MINUTES

INGREDIENTS

1 tbsp olive oil

1 red onion, diced

500 g / 1 lb lean beef mince

1 tsp chilli powder

1 tsp smoked paprika

1 tsp ground cumin

1 tsp ground coriander

400 g / 14 oz tinned chopped tomatoes

200 ml / 6 ½ fl. oz water

400 g / 14 oz tinned kidney beans, drained

200 g / 7 oz unsalted tortilla chips

50 g / 1 ¾ oz jalapeño peppers in brine

100 g / 3 ½ oz / 1 cup lighter Cheddar cheese, grated

100 g / 3 ½ oz / 1 cup lighter Red Leicester, grated

METHOD

1. Heat the oil over a medium high heat in a large casserole. Add the onion and cook for 5-10 minutes until softened. Add the beef mince and brown before adding the chilli powder, paprika, cumin and coriander. Fry for a further minute until fragrant before adding the chopped tomatoes and water. Bring to the boil and then reduce to a simmer and cover and cook for 45 minutes, adding the beans for the last 10 minutes.

2. Preheat the oven to 180°C (160°C fan) / 350F / gas 4. Put the tortilla chips in a cast iron skillet or oven proof dish, top with a generous helping of the chilli, jalapeños and grated cheese before placing in the oven.

3. Bake for 10-15 minutes so that the cheese has melted and started to brown.

4. Serve with guacamole and fresh salsa.

Baked chicken with couscous

SERVES: 4 | PREP TIME: 15 MINUTES | COOKING TIME: 10 MINUTES

INGREDIENTS

2 chicken breasts

1 tbsp olive oil

1 tsp paprika

1 tsp honey

1 lemon, juiced

100 g / 3 ½ oz / ½ cup couscous

150 ml / 5 ¼ fl. oz / ⅔ cup reduced salt chicken stock, boiling

parsley, chopped

½ cucumber, sliced

2 red chillies (chilis), deseeded and sliced

METHOD

1. Preheat the oven to 200°C (180°C fan) / 400F / gas 6.

2. Trim the chicken breast to remove any fat, roughly chop into bite sized pieces.

3. Place the chicken into a mixing bowl with the oil, paprika, honey and lemon juice. Season with salt and black pepper and toss to coat.

4. Place the chicken onto a baking tray and roast in the oven for 15 minutes.

5. Place the couscous into a bowl. Pour the stock into the bowl and cover with a plate. Leave for 5 minutes at which point the couscous should have absorbed the liquid.

6. Combine the chicken with the couscous and mix through the parsley. Season with salt and black pepper to taste.

7. Serve the chicken and couscous with the cucumber and sliced chillies on the side.

Chunky bacon and vegetable soup

SERVES: 4 | PREP TIME: 5 MINUTES | COOKING TIME: 20 MINUTES

INGREDIENTS

2 tbsp olive oil

2 tbsp butter

1 onion, finely chopped

2 cloves of garlic, crushed

2 medium potatoes, cubed

3 carrots, cubed

1 litre / 1 pint 15 fl. oz / 4 cups vegetable stock

150 g / 5 ½ oz / 1 cup peas, defrosted if frozen

4 rashers streaky bacon

a few sprigs of chervil to serve

METHOD

1. Heat the oil and butter in a saucepan and fry the onion for 5 minutes or until softened.

2. Add the garlic, potatoes and carrots to the pan and cook for 2 more minutes, then stir in the vegetable stock and bring to the boil.

3. Simmer for 12 minutes then add the peas and simmer for a further 5 minutes.

4. While the peas are cooking, cook the bacon under a hot grill until crispy then chop into large pieces.

5. Stir the bacon into the soup, add salt and pepper to taste and garnish with chervil.

Salmon pies

SERVES: 4 | PREP TIME: 5 MINUTES | COOKING TIME: 30 MINUTES

INGREDIENTS

2 tbsp low-fat butter

1 tsp plain (all-purpose) flour

250 ml / 9 fl. oz / 1 cup skimmed milk

200 g / 7 oz salmon fillet, cubed

250 g / 9 oz light puff pastry

1 egg, beaten

METHOD

1. Preheat the oven to 200°C (180° fan) / 400F / gas 6. Meanwhile, heat the butter in a saucepan then stir in the flour and cook for 30 seconds.

2. Gradually pour in the milk, stirring continuously, then bring to a gentle simmer. Once thickened, take off the heat and stir for another minute.

3. Stir in the salmon, then season with salt and black pepper and divide the mixture between 4 small pie dishes. Roll out the light puff pastry on a floured surface and cut out 4 circles.

4. Top each pie dish with a pastry lid and press around the edges to seal. Brush the tops of the pastry with beaten egg then bake for 25 minutes or until the pastry is golden brown and puffy.

Cauliflower and pea gratin

SERVES: 2 | PREP TIME: 15 MINUTES | COOKING TIME: 40 MINUTES

INGREDIENTS

75 g / 2 ½ oz / ⅓ cup light butter spread

2 cloves of garlic, minced

1 head of cauliflower, florets only

100 g / 3 ½ oz / ⅔ cup garden peas

350 ml / 11 ¾ fl. oz / 1 ½ cups lighter double (heavy) cream

100 g / 3 ½ oz / 1 cup lighter cheddar cheese, grated

METHOD

1. Preheat the oven to 180°C (160°C fan) / 350F / gas 4.

2. Combine the butter spread and the garlic. Rub the inside of an ovenproof dish with the garlic and butter mixture.

3. Place the cauliflower and peas into the dish before pouring over the cream. Season with salt and black pepper.

4. Top the dish with the grated cheese and place onto a baking tray.

5. Transfer to the oven and bake for 40 minutes at which point the cheese will have melted and the cauliflower should be softened.

6. Remove and serve hot with a side salad.

Bruschetta with ham

SERVES: 1 | PREP TIME: 10 MINUTES

INGREDIENTS

2 slices of sourdough bread, toasted

1 tsp wholegrain mustard

1 lemon, juiced

2 tsp extra virgin olive oil

1 tomato sliced

½ white onion, sliced

1 green chilli (chili), sliced

80 g / 3 oz Bresaola ham

METHOD

1. Place the bread onto a serving plate. Combine the mustard, lemon juice and oil and whisk together before drizzling over the toasted bread.

2. Arrange the sliced tomato, onion and chilli on top of the bruschetta before topping with the ham and a little seasoning.

Beef and butterbean stew

SERVES: 6 | PREP TIME: 5 MINUTES | COOKING TIME: 3 HOURS, 15 MINUTES

INGREDIENTS

4 tbsp olive oil

800 g / 1 lb 12 oz braising steak, diced

1 onion, finely chopped

4 cloves of garlic, finely chopped

400 g / 14 oz / 2 cups canned tomatoes, chopped

400 ml / 14 fl. oz / 1 ⅔ cups good quality beef stock

400 g / 14 oz / 2 cups canned butter beans, drained

1 head of broccoli, broken into florets

METHOD

1. Preheat the oven to 140°C (120° fan) / 275F / gas 1. Heat half of the oil in a large cast iron casserole dish and sear the beef on all sides until well browned.

2. Remove the meat from the pan, add the rest of the oil and fry the onions and garlic for 5 minutes. Add the tomatoes and stock and bring to a simmer then return the beef to the pan. Cover the casserole with a lid, transfer it to the oven and cook for 3 hours.

3. Around 30 minutes before the end of the cooking time, stir in the butter beans and broccoli and season.

4. Ladle into bowls and top with a spoonful of fresh tomato and chilli relish.

Thai red vegetable curry

SERVES: 2 | PREP TIME: 20 MINUTES | COOKING TIME: 30 MINUTES

INGREDIENTS

1 tsp groundnut oil

2 tbsp Thai red curry paste

1 aubergine (eggplant), diced

1 squash, peeled and diced

75 g / 2 ½ oz cherry tomatoes, halved

2 kaffir lime leaves

1 stick lemongrass, bruised

1 tbsp fish sauce

coriander stalks, chopped, and leaves

400 ml / 14 fl. oz / 1 ¾ cups low-fat coconut milk

METHOD

1. In a large wok, heat the oil over a medium high heat. Add the curry paste and fry for 1 – 2 minutes until fragrant.

2. Add the aubergine, squash, cherry tomatoes, lime leaves, lemongrass, fish sauce and chopped coriander stalks continuing to fry for a further 2 minutes. If the pan is a little dry add a splash of the coconut milk.

3. Pour in the coconut milk and bring to the boil and then reduce to a simmer for 12-15 minutes.

4. Serve in a bowl and garnish with the chopped coriander leaves.

Cauliflower and bulgur wheat casserole

SERVES: 2-4 | PREP TIME: 20 MINUTES | COOKING TIME: 1 HOUR

INGREDIENTS

1 tbsp olive oil

1 onion, diced

2 cloves of garlic, chopped

1 tsp paprika

1 tsp turmeric

1 tsp chilli (chili) flakes

1 tbsp tomato purée

1 head of cauliflower, florets only

200 g / 7 oz bulgur wheat, rinsed

500 ml / 17 fl. oz / 2 cups reduced salt
vegetable stock

parsley, chopped

METHOD

1. Heat the olive oil in a large heavy casserole pan over a medium heat. Add the onions and cook for 5-6 minutes until softened. Add the garlic and cook for a further minute until fragrant.

2. Add the spices to the pan followed by the cauliflower. Stir to coat the cauliflower with the spices and oil.

3. Add the bulgur wheat to the pan and stir before adding the stock to the pan. Heat until boiling before reducing to a simmer. Place the lid on top and leave to cook gradually for 40-45 minutes.

4. Before serving mix the parsley through the casserole and season with salt and black pepper to taste.

Pasta alla norma

SERVES: 2 | PREP TIME: 10 MINUTES | COOKING TIME: 40 MINUTES

INGREDIENTS

low calorie cooking spray

1 onion, diced

1 clove of garlic, thinly sliced

pinch of chilli (chili) flakes

1 aubergine (eggplant), chopped

fresh basil, roughly chopped

400 g / 14 oz canned chopped tomatoes

120 g / 4 ¼ oz whole wheat spaghetti

50 g / 1 ¾ oz / ½ cup low-fat salad cheese, crumbled

METHOD

1. Heat the oil in a pan over a medium heat. Add the onion and cook for 5 minutes until softened, add the garlic and chilli flakes and cook for a further minute.

2. Add the aubergine and most of the basil and tomatoes to the pan, cover and turn down to a simmer. Cook for 20 minutes until you have a thick tomato sauce, season to taste.

3. Bring a pan of salted water to the boil and add the pasta. Cook for 12-15 minutes until soft, drain and add to the pan with the tomato sauce.

4. To serve, spoon the pasta and sauce onto a plate and sprinkle over the cheese and garnish with the remaining basil.

Lamb shank tagine

SERVES: 4 | PREP TIME: 5 MINUTES | COOKING TIME: 2 HOURS

INGREDIENTS

4 lamb shanks

12 baby carrots, peeled

8 spring onions, trimmed

4 small turnips, peeled

6 new potatoes, peeled and halved

400 ml / 14 fl. oz / 1 ⅔ cups lamb stock

2 cloves of garlic, crushed

1 lemon, juiced

flat leaf parsley, chopped

METHOD

1. Preheat the oven to 180°C (160° fan) / 350F / gas 4.

2. Put each lamb shank in an individual tagine and divide the vegetables between them.

3. Mix the lamb stock with the garlic and lemon juice and season well with salt and pepper, then pour it over the lamb and put on the lids.

4. Transfer the tagines to the oven and bake for 2 hours.

5. Remove the lids and sprinkle with parsley before serving.

Roast vegetable pizza

MAKES: 1 | PREP TIME: 15 MINUTES | COOKING TIME: 35 MINUTES

INGREDIENTS

100 g / 3 ½ oz / ⅔ cup strong white flour

100 g / 3 ½ oz / ⅔ cup strong wholewheat flour

1 tsp easy-blend dried yeast

a pinch of salt

125ml / 4 fl. oz warm water

1 tsp olive oil

½ red onion, roughly chopped

1 courgette (zucchini), sliced

1 pepper, deseeded and sliced

100 g / 3 ½ oz mushrooms, roughly chopped

4 garlic cloves, lightly crushed

1 tsp each of oregano, basil and chilli (chili flakes)

1 tbsp low-fat pesto

150 g / 5 oz ricotta cheese

1 egg

METHOD

1. Preheat oven to 180°C (160°C fan) / 350F / gas 4. Combine the flours, yeast and salt in bowl of a stand mixer. Mix using the dough hook, gradually add the water and oil until a soft dough forms.

2. Knead on a floured surface for a further minute, place into a lightly oiled bowl and cover with cling film to prove.

3. Combine the chopped vegetables, garlic, oregano, basil and chilli flakes with a drizzle of oil. Toss to coat and place onto a baking tray in the oven for 15-20 minutes until softened and slightly charred and remove.

4. Turn the heat up to 240°C (220°C fan) / 475F / gas 9. Turn out the dough and knock it back. Roll out to the desired shape and toss the vegetables with the pesto. Top the pizza dough with the roasted vegetables and add the ricotta, break the egg into the centre of the pizza.

5. Place into the oven on a baking tray for 15 minutes until the base is crisp and the cheese has started to brown.

Lamb and summer veg stew

SERVES: 4 | PREP TIME: 5 MINUTES | COOKING TIME: 1 HOUR, 15 MINUTES

INGREDIENTS

4 tbsp olive oil

450 g / 1 lb lamb leg, cubed

1 onion, diced

3 cloves of garlic, finely chopped

200 g / 7 oz / 1 cup canned tomatoes, chopped

600 ml / 1 pint / 2 ½ cups good quality lamb stock

½ Japanese aubergine (eggplant), sliced

2 courgettes (zucchini), cubed

150 g / 5 ½ oz green (string) beans

flat leaf parsley to serve

METHOD

1. Heat half of the oil in a large saucepan and sear the lamb on all sides until well browned.

2. Remove the lamb from the pan, add the rest of the oil and fry the onions and garlic for 5 minutes.

3. Add the tomatoes and stock and bring to a simmer then return the lamb to the pan.

4. Cover the pan with a lid and simmer gently for 45 minutes.

5. Add the aubergine, courgette and beans and simmer for a further 15 minutes then taste the sauce for seasoning and adjust with salt and pepper.

6. Garnish with parsley just before serving.

Creamy pea soup

SERVES: 4 | PREP TIME: 5 MINUTES | COOKING TIME: 15 MINUTES

INGREDIENTS

2 tbsp olive oil

2 tbsp low-fat butter

1 onion, finely chopped

2 garlic cloves, crushed

400 g / 14 oz peas, defrosted if frozen

1 litre / 1 pint 15 fl. oz / 4 cups vegetable stock

100 ml / 3 ½ fl. oz / ½ cup light cream

1 tbsp mint leaves, finely chopped

METHOD

1. Heat the oil and butter in a saucepan and fry the onion for 5 minutes or until softened.

2. Add the garlic and peas to the pan and cook for 2 more minutes, then stir in the vegetable stock and bring to the boil.

3. Simmer for 5 minutes then stir in the double cream and mint.

4. Blend the soup until smooth with a liquidizer or immersion blender then try the soup and adjust the seasoning with salt and pepper.

5. Ladle into warm bowls and sprinkle with black pepper.

Fusilli puttanesca

SERVES: 1 | PREP TIME: 10 MINUTES | COOKING TIME: 15 MINUTES

INGREDIENTS

75 g / 2 ½ oz fusilli pasta

1 tbsp olive oil

1 shallot, finely chopped

1 clove of garlic, minced

1 tsp chilli (chili) flakes

200 g / 7 oz passata

180 g / 6 ½ oz tinned tuna, in spring water

a handful of black olives, halved and deseeded

1 tbsp capers

Parmesan or Pecorino cheese, to garnish

METHOD

1. Bring a pan of salted water to the boil, add the pasta and cook for 10-12 minutes until cooked slightly al dente. Drain and set aside.

2. Heat the oil over a medium heat in a frying pan. Add the shallot and cook for 1 minute before adding the garlic and cooking for a further 30 seconds. Add the chilli, passata, tuna, olives and capers to the pan and simmer for 4-5 minutes until fragrant.

3. Add the pasta to your serving plate and spoon over the tuna sauce, garnish with a little grated cheese.

95

Red onion savoury cheesecake

SERVES: 6-8 | PREP TIME: 25 MINUTES | COOKING TIME: 40-50 MINUTES

INGREDIENTS

200 g / 7 oz light puff pastry

3 tbsp olive oil

3 red onions, halved and sliced

450 g / 1 lb / 2 cups cream cheese

100 g / 3 ½ oz soft blue cheese, cubed

50 g / 1 ¾ oz / ½ cup pistachio nuts, chopped

METHOD

1. Preheat the oven to 220°C (200° fan) / 425F / gas 7 and grease a baking tray.

2. Roll out the pastry on a lightly floured surface. Invert a large loaf tin on top of the pastry and cut round it, then transfer the pastry to the baking tray and prick with a fork.

3. Bake the pastry for 15 minutes or until golden brown and cooked through. Leave to cool.

4. Heat the oil in a large sauté pan and fry the onions over a gentle heat for 20 minutes, stirring occasionally.

5. Line the loaf tin with cling film then spoon in the onions and level the top.

6. Beat the cream cheese with the blue cheese and half of the pistachio nuts and spread it over the onions, then scatter over the rest of the pistachios.

7. Put the pastry on top, press down firmly and cover with cling film, then chill in the fridge for 3 hours before unmoulding and slicing.

Mexican baked eggs

SERVES: 4 | PREP TIME: 15 MINUTES | COOKING TIME: 30 MINUTES

INGREDIENTS

2 tbsp olive oil

1 onion, diced

2 red chillies (chilies), deseeded and finely chopped

2 red peppers, deseeded finely sliced

1 tsp smoked paprika

1 tsp cayenne powder

1 tsp cumin powder

200 g / 7 oz mushrooms, sliced

400 g / 14 oz chopped tomatoes, canned

400 g / 14 oz tin of kidney beans, drained

3 wholemeal tortilla wraps

300 ml / 10 fl. oz low-fat soured cream

4 free range eggs

METHOD

1. Preheat oven to 180°C (160°C fan) / 350F / gas 4. In a pan, heat half the oil over a medium high heat, frying the onion for 3-4 minutes until translucent. Add the chillies, frying for a minute before adding the pepper, paprika, cayenne, cumin and mushrooms. Cook for a further 3 minutes, before adding the tomatoes. Turn down to a simmer and cook for 15 minutes, adding the beans for the final 5 minutes.

2. In a large ovenproof pan, heat the remaining oil. Fry each tortilla wrap for a minute on each side until browned. Remove from the heat and arrange all three in the pan. Spoon the tomato and bean mixture into the pan leaving room at the top.

3. Pour the soured cream over the top, ensuring a level surface, before cracking the eggs on top. Place in the oven for 10 minutes or until the eggs are cooked. Remove from the oven and garnish with fresh chilli and coriander.

Steak stew

SERVES: 4 | PREP TIME: 5 MINUTES | COOKING TIME: 1 HOUR, 45 MINUTES

INGREDIENTS

2 tbsp olive oil

1 onion, finely chopped

1 carrot, finely chopped

1 celery stick, finely chopped

1 red chilli (chili), finely chopped

2 cloves of garlic, crushed

½ tsp cayenne pepper

450 g / 1 lb / 2 cups braising steak, cubed

400 g / 14 oz / 1 ⅔ cups beef stock

400 g / 14 oz / 1 ¾ cups canned
kidney beans, drained

400 g / 14 oz / 1 ¾ cups canned sweetcorn, drained

2 courgettes (zucchini), sliced

METHOD

1. Heat the oil in a large saucepan and fry the onion, carrot, celery and chilli for 3 minutes, stirring occasionally.

2. Add the garlic and cayenne and cook for 2 minutes, then add the beef.

3. Fry the beef until it starts to brown then add the stock and bring to a gentle simmer.

4. Cook for 1 hour, stirring occasionally, then add the kidney beans, sweetcorn and courgette and cook for a further 30 minutes. Taste for seasoning.

Vegetable pizza

SERVES: 2 | PREP TIME: 2 HOURS, 30 MINUTES | COOKING TIME: 10-12 MINUTES

INGREDIENTS

400 g / 14 oz / 2 ⅔ cups strong white bread flour

½ tsp easy blend dried yeast

2 tsp caster (superfine) sugar

1 tsp fine sea salt

1 tbsp olive oil

4 tbsp tomato pizza sauce

½ aubergine (eggplant), chopped

1 courgette (zucchini), chopped

1 red pepper, chopped

1 yellow pepper, chopped

100 g / 3 ½ oz preserved artichokes, chopped

150 g / 5 ½ oz mozzarella, grated

2 tsp dried oregano

METHOD

1. Mix together the flour, yeast, sugar and salt and stir the oil into 140 ml of warm water.

2. Stir the liquid into the dry ingredients then knead on a lightly oiled surface for 10 minutes or until smooth and elastic.

3. Leave the dough to rest covered with oiled cling film for 1-2 hours until doubled in size. Preheat the oven to 220°C (200° fan) / 425F/ gas 7 and grease 2 non-stick baking trays.

4. Knead the dough for 2 more minutes then divide in half and roll out into 2 circles.

5. Transfer the bases to the baking trays, spread with pizza sauce and sprinkle with cheese. Arrange the vegetables on top and sprinkle with oregano then bake for 10-12 minutes.

Tuna bruschetta

SERVES: 1 | PREP TIME: 10 MINUTES

INGREDIENTS

180 g / 6 ½ oz tuna, tinned in water

1 tsp capers, chopped

2 spring onions (scallions), chopped

1 lemon, juice and zest

1 tsp extra virgin olive oil

2 slices of ciabatta or baguette, toasted

1 garlic clove, peeled

fresh parsley, chopped

METHOD

1. In a bowl, mix together the tuna, capers, spring onions, lemon and olive oil. Combine fully and season with salt and black pepper to taste.

2. Rub the toasted bread with the garlic clove to flavour.

3. Top with the tuna mixture and chopped parsley before serving.

Chicken burger

SERVES: 2 | PREP TIME: 10 MINUTES | COOKING TIME: 15 MINUTES

INGREDIENTS

2 tbsp sunflower oil

2 chicken breast fillets

1 egg, beaten

50 g / 1 ¾ oz / ⅓ cup panko breadcrumbs

1 tbsp low-fat mayonnaise

½ lemon, juiced

1 tsp fresh dill, chopped

a pinch of salt

2 seeded burger buns

METHOD

1. Preheat the oven to 180°C (160°C fan) / 350F / gas 4.

2. In a large frying pan, heat the oil over a medium high heat. Dip the chicken fillets into the beaten egg and then roll in the breadcrumbs until coated. Place the fillets into the heated oil and fry lightly on both sides until slightly golden. Remove from the pan and place onto a baking tray and bake in the oven for 10 minutes.

3. Combine the mayonnaise, lemon juice, dill and salt. Place the cooked chicken into the buns and top with the flavoured mayonnaise.

103

Spaghetti with stuffed tomato

SERVES: 2 | PREP TIME: 15 MINUTES | COOKING TIME: 30 MINUTES

INGREDIENTS

4 large firm tomatoes

small bunch of basil, chopped

1 clove of garlic, minced

50 g / 1 ¾ oz / ½ cup low-fat ricotta

1 courgette (zucchini), grated

1 tbsp capers

½ lemon, juice and zest

50 g / 1 ¾ oz / ½ cup Parmesan cheese, grated

2 tbsp panko breadcrumbs

120 g / 4 ¼ oz spaghetti

METHOD

1. Preheat the oven to 180°C (160°C fan) / 350F / gas 4.

2. Cut the top off the tomatoes and scoop out the pulp, set aside for later. Place the tomatoes cut side down on some kitchen paper to drain.

3. Mix the basil, garlic, ricotta, courgette, capers and lemon juice in a bowl and season with salt and black pepper.

4. In a separate bowl mix the lemon zest, cheese and breadcrumbs.

5. Spoon the ricotta mixture into the tomatoes and then top with the breadcrumbs. Place into a baking tray and transfer to the oven. Bake for 18-20 minutes until golden on top, remove and set aside.

6. Cook the pasta as per the packet instructions, drain and mix through the reserved tomato pulp and any filling that was not used.

7. Serve the pasta with the stuffed tomatoes on top. Sprinkle with the Parmesan.

Hawaii flatbread pizza

SERVES: 2 | PREP TIME: 1 HOUR | COOKING TIME: 15 MINUTES

INGREDIENTS

100 g / 3 ½ oz / ⅔ cup strong white flour

100 g / 3 ½ oz / ⅔ cup whole wheat flour

1 tsp easy-blend dried yeast

125 ml / 4 fl. oz / ¾ cup warm water

100 ml / 3 ½ fl. oz / ½ cup passata

200 g / 7 oz / 2 cups lighter Cheddar cheese, grated

200 g / 7 oz pineapple chunks

150 g / 5 ¼ oz chicken breast, cooked

100 g / 3 ½ oz fat free natural yogurt

1 lime, juiced

1 clove of garlic, minced

flat leaf parsley, chopped

METHOD

1. Combine the flours, yeast and a pinch of salt in a bowl. Pour in the water and knead for 5 minutes to create a springy dough. Roll out on a floured surface to the desired shape and place onto an oiled baking tray. Cover and leave to prove for 45 minutes in a warm place.

2. Preheat the oven to 220°C (200°C fan) / 425F / gas 7.

3. Spoon the passata onto the pizza bases and spread evenly over the surface. Top with the cheese, pineapple and chicken breast. Season with salt and black pepper before placing into the hot oven for 12-15 minutes until crisp and golden.

4. Combine the yogurt, lime juice and garlic before seasoning to taste.

5. Drizzle the yogurt over the cooked pizzas and scatter over the parsley.

Frittata
with courgette

SERVES: 4-6 | PREP TIME: 20 MINUTES | COOKING TIME: 40 MINUTES

INGREDIENTS

100 g / 3 ½ oz potatoes, peeled and diced

low calorie cooking spray

1 onion, diced

1 clove of garlic, chopped

1 courgette (zucchini), sliced

4 large eggs

100 ml / 3 ⅓ fl. oz / ½ cup low-fat soured cream

175 g / 6 oz / 1 ¾ cups lighter Cheddar cheese, grated

small bunch of flat leaf parsley, chopped

METHOD

1. Place the potatoes into a pan of salted boiled water and cook for 12-15 minutes until softened. Drain and set aside to cool.

2. Preheat the oven to 190°C (170°C fan) / 375F / gas 5.

3. Spray an ovenproof frying pan with cooking oil and place onto a medium heat. Add the onions and cook for 4-5 minutes until softened before adding the garlic and courgette. Cooking for a further 2-3 minutes turning the courgettes in the pan to brown on both sides.

4. Stir in the potato and cook for a couple more minutes.

5. Beat together the eggs, soured cream, cheese and season with salt and black pepper. Pour into the potato and onion and mix through the parsley.

6. Transfer to the oven and bake in the oven for 30-35 minutes until the top has browned and the mixture has set.

7. Remove from the oven to cool before placing a plate on top and turning out.

Mini chicken and vegetable pies

SERVES: 4 | PREP TIME: 45 MINUTES | COOKING TIME: 45 MINUTES

INGREDIENTS

2 tbsp butter

1 onion, chopped

1 potato, chopped

1 tsp plain (all-purpose) flour

250 ml / 9 fl. oz / 1 cup milk

200 g / 7 oz cooked chicken breast, cubed

75 g / 2 ½ oz / ½ cup peas, defrosted if frozen

75 g / 2 ½ oz / 1 cup button mushrooms, quartered

6 cherry tomatoes, quartered

FOR THE PASTRY

100 g / 3 ½ oz / ½ cup butter, cubed and chilled

200 g / 7 oz / 1 ⅓ cups plain (all-purpose) flour

METHOD

1. To make the pastry, rub the butter into the flour until the mixture resembles fine breadcrumbs. Stir in just enough cold water to bring the pastry together into a pliable dough then chill for 30 minutes.

2. Preheat the oven to 200°C (180° fan) / 400F / gas 6. Heat the butter in a saucepan and fry the onion and potato for 5 minutes without colouring. Sprinkle in the flour, then stir in the milk and bubble until it thickens slightly.

3. Add the chicken, peas, mushrooms and tomatoes to the pan and heat through, then season to taste.

4. Roll out the pastry on a floured surface and cut out 4 circles. Divide the filling between four pie dishes and brush the rims with water. Top each pie with a pastry lid and crimp the edges to seal. Bake the pies for 25 minutes.

Pan-fried sea bass with Chinese artichokes

SERVES: 4 | PREP TIME: 25 MINUTES | COOKING TIME: 40-50 MINUTES

INGREDIENTS

½ butternut squash, cut into chunks

200 g / 7 oz Chinese artichokes, scrubbed

2 tbsp olive oil

4 portions of sea bass fillet

2 tbsp butter

2 courgettes (zucchini), cut into chunks

100 g / 3 ½ oz chestnut mushrooms, halved

50 g / 1 ¾ oz / ⅓ cup walnuts

METHOD

1. Preheat the oven to 180°C (160° fan) / 350F / gas 4 and put a roasting tin in to heat.

2. Boil the butternut squash in salted water for 3 minutes, then add the Chinese artichokes and cook for a further 4 minutes. Drain well.

3. Heat the oil in a frying pan and fry the sea bass skin side down for 3 minutes. Transfer the fillets, skin side up to the roasting tin in the oven and cook for 5 minutes.

4. Meanwhile, put the frying pan back on the hob and add the butter.

5. Fry the drained squash and artichokes with the courgette and mushrooms for 5 minutes, then stir in the walnuts and season. Divide the vegetables between four warm plates and top each one with a portion of sea bass.

Beef in red wine

SERVES: 2 | PREP TIME: 15 MINUTES | COOKING TIME: 1 HOUR, 15 MINUTES

INGREDIENTS

1 tbsp olive oil

450 g / 15 oz extra lean beef, diced

flour for dusting

1 onion, diced

2 garlic cloves, minced

150 ml / 5 fl. oz red wine

150 ml / 5 fl. oz beef stock

2 bay leaves

fresh thyme

METHOD

1. In a large casserole, heat the oil over a medium high heat. Season the beef and then brown in the oil. Remove with a slotted spoon at set aside, dusting with flour to catch the juices.

2. Add the onion to the pan and cook for 8 minutes until soft and translucent. Add the garlic and cook for a further minute before adding the wine to the pan. Allow this to bubble away until the liquid has reduced by half. Pour in the beef stock and return the beef to the pan with the bay leaves and thyme. Bring back to the boil and then reduce to a gentle simmer and cook for at least 1 hour, uncovered, until the beef is soft and the sauce has thickened.

Ham, cabbage and feta bake

SERVES: 4-6 | PREP TIME: 20 MINUTES | COOKING TIME: 45 MINUTES

INGREDIENTS

low calorie cooking spray

1 onion, diced

2 cloves of garlic, minced

3 potatoes, peeled and diced

1 savoy cabbage, shredded

250 ml / 9 fl. oz / 1 cup low salt vegetable stock

bunch of flat leaf parsley, chopped

200 g / 7 oz cooked ham, diced

200 g / 7 oz lighter Greek style
salad cheese, crumbled

75 g / 2 ½ oz / ⅔ cup walnut pieces

METHOD

1. Preheat the oven to 180°C (160°C fan) / 350F /
    gas 4. Place a heavy bottomed pan onto a
    medium heat and spray with cooking oil.
    Add the onion and fry for 4-5 minutes. Add
    the garlic and fry for a minute until fragrant.

2. Add the potatoes and cabbage to the pan
    and mix through the onions and garlic. Cook
    for 4-5 minutes.

3. Pour the stock into the pan and leave to
    bubble and cook for 12-15 minutes. Stir the
    parsley, half the ham and half the cheese
    through the cabbage and potato mixture
    before seasoning. Spoon this into an
    ovenproof dish before scattering over the
    remaining ham, cheese and the walnuts.

4. Bake in the oven for 25-30 minutes,
    until the top has browned.

115

Mini sausage cassoulet

SERVES: 6 | PREP TIME: 10 MINUTES | COOKING TIME: 1 HOUR, 45 MINUTES

INGREDIENTS

400 g / 14 oz / 2 ⅔ cups dried haricot beans, soaked overnight

3 litres / 5 pints 6 fl. oz / 12 cups chicken stock

2 tbsp olive oil

6 good quality pork sausages

1 morteau sausage, sliced

100 g / 3 ½ oz chorizo, cubed

2 cloves of garlic, crushed

50 g / 1 ¾ oz / ⅔ cup breadcrumbs

a few sprigs of parsley to garnish

METHOD

1. Put the beans in a large saucepan with the stock and simmer gently for 1 hour.

2. Meanwhile, heat the oil in a frying pan and brown the sausages all over, then cut them in half.

3. Preheat the oven to 150°C (130° fan) / 300F / gas 2.

4. Drain the beans and reserve the stock then stir in the sausages, morteau, chorizo and garlic.

5. Divide the mixture between 6 mini casserole dishes, then sprinkle with breadcrumbs.

6. Bake the cassoulets for 45 minutes, topping up with extra stock if necessary.

Penne rosa

SERVES: 2 | PREP TIME: 10 MINUTES | COOKING TIME: 20 MINUTES

INGREDIENTS

100 g / 3 ½ oz whole wheat penne

low calorie cooking spray

2 cloves of garlic, chopped

1 tsp chilli (chili) flakes

100 g / 3 ½ oz spinach, washed

400 g / 14 oz canned chopped tomatoes

75 g / 2 ½ oz low-fat ricotta cheese

METHOD

1. Place the pasta into a pan of salted boiling water and cook for 8-10 minutes until al dente. Drain and set aside.

2. Heat a large skillet over a medium heat and spray with oil. Add the garlic and chilli flakes and cook for 1 minute until fragrant. Add the spinach and wilt in the pan, pouring off any excess liquid taking care not to lose the garlic and chilli.

3. Add the pasta to the pan and toss through the spinach before adding the tomatoes. Leave to cook for a further 5 minutes mixing the pasta through the sauce, seasoning. Spoon into serving bowls and top with some ricotta cheese.

Chilli con carne

SERVES: 4 | PREP TIME: 10 MINUTES | COOKING TIME: 50 MINUTES

INGREDIENTS

1 tbsp olive oil

1 large onion, diced

2 red peppers, deseeded and diced

500 g / 1 lb lean beef mince

1 tsp chilli powder

1 tsp smoked paprika

1 tsp ground cumin

1 tsp ground coriander

400 g / 14 oz tinned chopped tomatoes

200 ml / 6 ½ fl. oz water

400 g / 14 oz tinned kidney beans, drained

low-fat soured cream

METHOD

1. Heat the oil over a medium high heat in a large casserole. Add the onion and peppers and cook for 5-10 minutes until softened. Add the beef mince and brown before adding the chilli powder, paprika, cumin and coriander. Fry for a further minute until fragrant before adding the chopped tomatoes and water. Bring to the boil and then reduce to a simmer and cover and cook for 45 minutes.

2. Add the kidney beans to the chilli around 10 minutes before serving to heat through.

3. Serve in a bowl topped with a large spoonful of soured cream.

Lentil stew with vegetables

SERVES: 2-4 | PREP TIME: 15 MINUTES | COOKING TIME: 45 MINUTES

INGREDIENTS

low calorie cooking spray

1 onion, diced

3 cloves of garlic, minced

2 large carrots, diced

2 potatoes, peeled and diced

1 tsp ground coriander (cilantro)

1 tsp ras-el-hanout

400 g / 14 oz canned chopped tomatoes

500 ml / 17 fl. oz / 2 cups low salt vegetable stock

400 g / 14 oz canned green lentils

200 g / 7 oz / 1 ⅓ cups frozen sweetcorn

200 g / 7 oz / 1 ⅓ cups frozen peas

fresh parsley, chopped

METHOD

1. Spray a casserole pan with the oil and place onto a medium heat. Add the onion and cook for 4-5 minutes until soft and translucent. Add the garlic and cook for a further minute until fragrant.

2. Add the carrots, potatoes, coriander and ras-el-hanout to the pan and mix through the onions for 1-2 minutes until you can smell the spices. Add a little more oil if necessary.

3. Add the tomatoes and stock to the pan and increase the heat until boiling. Reduce to a simmer before adding the lentils, sweetcorn and peas. Cover and leave to cook at a low simmer for 30-35 minutes, adding seasoning.

4. Just before serving mix through the parsley, reserving some to sprinkle over the surface.

Vegetable bean soup

SERVES: 2 | PREP TIME: 20 MINUTES | COOKING TIME: 20 MINUTES

INGREDIENTS

1 tbsp olive oil

2 echalion shallots, diced

1 celery sticks, finely sliced

1 carrots, diced

2 garlic cloves, minced

½ cauliflower, florets only

1 tsp herbes de Provence

750 ml / 25 fl. oz vegetable stock

1 bay leaf

240 g / 8 ½ oz can of cannellini beans, drained

4 slices of crusty wholemeal bread

30 g Parmesan, finely grated

METHOD

1. In a large saucepan or casserole dish, heat the oil over a medium high heat. Add the shallots, celery and carrots and cook for 4-5 minutes until fragrant and softened but not browned. Add the garlic, cauliflower and herbes de Provence and fry for a further 2 minutes until fragrant.

2. Pour in the stock, season and bring to the boil. Reduce the heat to a simmer and cover, cooking for 15 minutes before adding the beans. Cook for a further 5 minutes.

3. Toast one side of the bread under a grill before turning over and sprinkling over the parmesan. Grill the other side until the cheese has browned. Serve the hot soup in bowls with the Parmesan toast on the side and garnish with chopped fresh parsley.

Chicken in barbecue sauce

SERVES: 2 | PREP TIME: 10 MINUTES | COOKING TIME: 30 MINUTES

INGREDIENTS

100 g / 3 ½ oz low sugar ketchup

2 tbsp fruit syrup

1 clove of garlic, minced

1 tbsp Worcestershire sauce

1 tbsp cider vinegar

1 tbsp hot sauce

1 tsp smoked paprika

low calories cooking spray

2 chicken breasts, trimmed and cubed

200 g / 7 oz new potatoes

½ cucumber, sliced

100 g / 3 ½ oz cherry tomatoes, halved

METHOD

1. Preheat the oven to 200°C (180°C fan) / 400F / gas 6.

2. For the sauce, combine the first seven ingredients in a pan and heat gently, stirring continuously. Continue to cook for 8-10 minutes until the sauce thickens. Season to taste and keep warm.

3. Place the chicken onto a baking tray and spray with a little oil and season. Place into the oven and cook for 15 minutes until firm to the touch and slightly coloured at the edges. Place the potatoes into a pan of salted boiling water and cook for 18-20 minutes until softened. Drain and set aside.

4. Place the chicken onto serving plates and drizzle over the barbecue sauce. Add the potatoes and chopped cucumber and tomatoes to the plate before serving.

Mediterranean vegetable stew

SERVES: 2 | PREP TIME: 15 MINUTES | COOKING TIME: 45 MINUTES

INGREDIENTS

low calorie cooking spray

1 onion, diced

1 clove of garlic, chopped

120 g / 4 ¼ oz chestnut mushrooms, sliced

1 sweet pepper, sliced and deseeded

1 aubergine (eggplant), diced

1 tbsp tomato purée

1 tsp smoked paprika

1 tsp chilli (chili) flakes

50 g / 1 ¾ oz / ¼ cup sundried tomatoes

400 g / 14 oz chopped tomatoes

400 ml / 14 fl. oz / 1 ¾ cups low salt vegetable stock

fresh basil leaves, chopped

METHOD

1. Place a casserole pan onto a medium heat and spray with cooking oil.

2. Add the onions and cook for 5-6 minutes until softened. Add the garlic, mushrooms, pepper and aubergine to the pan and cook for a further 4-5 minutes to soften. Add more cooking spray as required. Add the tomato purée, paprika and chilli flakes to the pan and mix through the vegetables.

3. Add the sundried tomatoes, chopped tomatoes and stock to the pan. Increase the heat until boiling before covering and reducing to a simmer. Cook covered for 30 minutes until the vegetables have softened.

4. Season to taste before stirring through the basil and serving.

Mushroom casserole

SERVES: 2 | PREP TIME: 10 MINUTES | COOKING TIME: 40 MINUTES

INGREDIENTS

low calorie cooking spray

1 onion, diced

2 cloves of garlic, finely chopped

200 g / 7 oz chestnut mushrooms, sliced

2 courgettes (zucchini), sliced

1 tsp smoked paprika

1 tbsp tomato purée

400 ml / 14 fl. oz / 1 ¾ cups reduced salt vegetable stock

200 g / 7 oz new potatoes, peeled

1 bay leaf

1 tbsp dill, chopped

METHOD

1. Spray a casserole pan with the oil and place over a medium heat. Add the onions and cook for 4-5 minutes until softened.

2. Add the garlic, mushrooms and courgettes to the pan and cook for a further 5 minutes stirring regularly. Continue to cook until the mushrooms release their moisture.

3. Stir the paprika and tomato purée through the vegetables for a minute before adding the stock to the pan. Add the potatoes and bay leaves and heat until boiling.

4. Reduce to a simmer and cover. Leave to cook at a low simmer for 30 minutes until the potatoes are softened. Season with salt and pepper to taste. Serve in warmed bowl with the dill scattered over the top.

123

Beef stew

SERVES: 4 | PREP TIME: 15 MINUTES | COOKING TIME: 1 HOUR, 30 MINUTES

INGREDIENTS

low calorie cooking spray

800 g / 1 lb 12 oz extra lean beef, diced

flour for dusting

1 onion, diced

2 garlic cloves, minced

3 carrots, sliced

1 tbsp tomato paste

500 ml / 17 fl. oz / 2 cups reduced salt beef stock

2 bay leaves

fresh parsley, chopped

METHOD

1. Spray a large casserole with oil and place over a medium high heat. Season the beef and then brown in the oil. Remove with a slotted spoon at set aside, dusting with flour to catch the juices.

2. Add the onion to the pan and cook for 4-6 minutes until soft and translucent. Add the garlic and carrots and cook for a further 2-3 minutes before stirring through the tomato paste.

3. Pour in the beef stock into the pan and return the beef with the bay leaves. Heat until boiling and then reduce to a gentle simmer and cook for at least 1 hour, uncovered, until the beef is soft and the sauce has thickened. Season and mix the parsley through the stew.

Squash risotto

SERVES: 2-4 | PREP TIME: 10 MINUTES | COOKING TIME: 40 MINUTES

INGREDIENTS

low calorie cooking spray

1 onion, diced

1 butternut squash, peeled and chopped

2 cloves garlic, minced

2 tbsp low-fat butter spread

300 g / 10 ½ oz / 1 ½ cup Arborio risotto rice

150 ml / 5 ¼ fl. oz / ⅔ cup white wine

500 ml / 17 fl. oz / 2 cups reduced salt chicken stock, warm

50 g / 1 ¾ oz / ½ cup Parmesan cheese, grated

100 g / 3 ½ oz low-fat ricotta cheese

basil, chopped

METHOD

1. Spray some oil in a heavy bottomed lidded pan over a medium heat. Add the onion, squash and a pinch of salt and fry for 3-4 minutes. Add the garlic for a further minute.

2. Add the butter spread to the pan and the rice and stir through to coat the rice with the butter and oil. Turn the heat up a little and add the wine. Allow to cook and bubble for 5 minutes. Reduce to a medium heat.

3. Gradually add the stock to the rice, placing the lid on the pan after each addition. Check that the liquid has been absorbed each time before adding further stock. Season to taste.

4. Stir half the Parmesan and the ricotta through the risotto and seasoning.

125

Cook's Corner

Skinny Comfort Food
Light bites
and sides

Baked breaded chicken sandwich

SERVES: 1 | PREP TIME: 15 MINUTES | COOKING TIME: 30 MINUTES

INGREDIENTS

1 chicken breast

1 tbsp plain (all-purpose) flour

1 egg, beaten

2 tbsp panko breadcrumbs

1 multi-seed roll

1 tbsp low-fat mayonnaise

1 tbsp extra virgin olive oil

¼ cucumber, sliced

2 leaves of lettuce

1 tbsp walnut pieces

METHOD

1. Preheat the oven to 180°C (160°C fan) / 350F / gas 4.

2. Place the chicken between two piece of cling film and gently flatten with a rolling pin.

3. Season the flour with salt and black pepper. Place the chicken into the flour and turn over to coat, shake off any excess.

4. Dip the chicken in the egg and them the breadcrumbs coating it fully. Place onto a baking tray and bake for 25-30 minutes until golden and crisp.

5. Prepare the roll by cutting in half and spreading mayonnaise on the top piece and drizzling the bottom with oil.

6. Place the chicken into the roll and add the cucumber, lettuce and walnut pieces before serving.

Carrot and ginger soup

SERVES: 4-6 | PREP TIME: 20 MINUTES | COOKING TIME: 40 MINUTES

INGREDIENTS

low calorie cooking spray

1 onion, diced

6-8 carrots, peeled and diced

2 cloves of garlic, minced

1 in piece of root ginger, peeled and sliced

1 tsp turmeric

1 tbsp tomato purée

500 ml / 17 fl. oz / 2 cups low salt vegetable stock

METHOD

1. Place a large casserole pan onto a medium heat. Spray with oil and add the onions, cooking for 4-5 minutes until softened.

2. Add the carrots to the pan and cook for a further 3-4 minutes before adding the garlic and ginger. Cook for a further minute until fragrant.

3. Stir the turmeric and tomato purée through the vegetables before adding the stock to the pan. Increase the heat until boiling before turning back down to a simmer and covering.

4. Cook for 30 minutes until the vegetables are tender. Blend the soup until smooth using a hand blender and season. Serve immediately or leave to cool and store in an airtight container for up to 5 days.

Rocket, pear and bacon salad

SERVES: 1 | PREP TIME: 10 MINUTES

INGREDIENTS

4 rashers of streaky bacon, fat removed

75 g / 2 ½ oz rocket (arugula)

50 g / 1 ¾ oz radicchio, sliced

1 pear, ripe

1 tsp honey

1 tbsp extra virgin olive oil

1 tbsp white wine vinegar

METHOD

1. Place a non-stick frying pan on a medium high heat. Add the bacon and cook for 8-10 minutes turning occasionally until cooked through. Remove and set aside to cool.

2. Place the rocket and radicchio onto a plate and mix together.

3. Core the pear and thinly slice.

4. Add the pear and bacon to the leaves.

5. Combine the honey, oil and vinegar and drizzle over the salad before seasoning with salt and black pepper.

Gammon and onion skewers

SERVES: 4 | PREP TIME: 20 MINUTES | COOKING TIME: 8 MINUTES

INGREDIENTS

6 salad onions

400 g / 14 oz unsmoked gammon, cubed

4 tbsp barbecue sauce

METHOD

1. Put 12 wooden skewers in a bowl of water and leave to soak for 20 minutes.

2. Meanwhile, cut off the green parts of the onions and reserve for garnish. Cut the bulb of the onions in half.

3. Thread the gammon and onions onto the skewers and spread them out on a large grill tray.

4. Brush them with barbecue sauce then grill for 4 minutes on each side or until the onions are slightly charred on the edges.

5. Slice the reserved onion greens on the diagonal and scatter over the skewers.

Nacho dip

SERVES: 4 | PREP TIME: 15 MINUTES

INGREDIENTS

2 red chillies (chili)

½ red onion

3 ripe avocados

2 garlic cloves, minced

1 bunch fresh coriander (cilantro)

6 cherry tomatoes

2 limes, juice and zest

Himalayan sea salt

METHOD

1. De-seed and finely chop the red chillies and finely dice the red onion.

2. Peel and de-stone the avocado and mash in a bowl with the back of a fork. Mix in the chopped chilli, garlic and onion.

3. Finely chop some of the coriander stalks and roughly chop the leaves before adding to the avocado along with the chopped and deseeded tomatoes. Add the lime juice and zest and season to taste with the salt.

4. Serve alongside plain tortilla chips for a great snack.

133

Seafood and avocado cocktails

SERVES: 5 | PREP TIME: 20 MINUTES

INGREDIENTS

250 g / 9 oz sashimi-grade tuna loin, diced

2 tbsp soy sauce

1 tsp sesame oil

4 avocados, halved and stoned

2 limes, juiced

1 tsp wasabi paste

150 g / 5 ½ oz cooked crayfish tails, peeled

150 g / 5 ½ oz / ¾ cup white crabmeat

18 king prawns

250 g / 9 oz / 1 cup light mayonnaise

2 tbsp fresh dill, chopped

cayenne pepper for sprinkling

METHOD

1. Toss the tuna with the soy and sesame oil then divide between 6 glasses.

2. Scrape the avocado flesh out of the skins and put it in a food processor with the lime juice and wasabi paste. Blend to a smooth puree and add salt to taste.

3. Spoon the avocado mixture on top of the tuna and top with the crayfish tails and crabmeat.

4. Arrange 3 king prawns on top of each cocktail, then pipe or spoon some mayonnaise on top. Sprinkle with dill and cayenne pepper and garnish with some extra sprigs of dill.

Aubergines with olives and feta

SERVES: 1 | PREP TIME: 10 MINUTES | COOKING TIME: 20 MINUTES

INGREDIENTS

1 aubergine (eggplant)

50 g / 1 ¾ oz / ⅓ cup Kalamata olives, pitted

75 g / 2 ½ oz reduced fat Greek salad cheese

1 tbsp olive oil

parsley, chopped

METHOD

1. Preheat the oven to 180°C (160°C fan) / 350F / gas 4.

2. Slice the aubergine in half lengthways before making incisions in the flesh along the full length of each half, taking care not to pierce the skin.

3. Halve the olives if large and cut the cheese into slices. Stuff the olives and cheese into the grooves in the aubergine.

4. Drizzle the oil the top of the stuffed aubergine and season with salt and black pepper. Place into an ovenproof dish and transfer to the oven. Bake for 20 minutes until the aubergine is tender. Garnish with some of the chopped parsley before serving.

Traditional stuffed tomatoes

SERVES: 4 | PREP TIME: 10-15 MINUTES | COOKING TIME: 15-20 MINUTES

INGREDIENTS

6 large vine tomatoes

600 g / 1 lb 5 oz / 4 cups beef mince

2 tbsp sunflower oil

2 cloves of garlic, minced

1 tsp dried oregano

1 tsp dried basil

250 g / 9 oz / 1 ½ cups cooked white long grain rice

oregano to garnish

METHOD

1. Preheat the oven to 190°C (170° fan) / 375F / gas 5.

2. Heat the sunflower oil in a large sauté pan set over a moderate heat. Sauté the garlic for 30 seconds before adding the beef mince. Cook until browned all over before adding the dried herbs and seasoning to taste.

3. Set to one side to cool as you prepare the tomatoes. Remove the tops and reserve to one side before scooping out the insides. Fill with the beef mince and replace the tops.

4. Spoon the rice into an oval baking dish and sprinkle with cold water. Sit the stuffed tomatoes on top and bake for 10-12 minutes until warmed through. Garnish with oregano before serving.

Roast pumpkin salad

SERVES: 2 | PREP TIME: 15 MINUTES | COOKING TIME: 40 MINUTES

INGREDIENTS

½ pumpkin, sliced

1 tbsp olive oil

1 tsp turmeric

½ tsp cayenne

½ tsp paprika

75 g / 2 ½ oz lighter mozzarella

50 g / 1 ¾ oz / ½ cup walnuts, chopped

METHOD

1. Preheat the oven to 180°C (160°C fan) / 350F / gas 4.

2. Place the slices of pumpkin into a roasting tray and scatter over the oil, turmeric, cayenne, paprika and season with salt and black pepper. Toss to coat the pumpkin with the spices.

3. Roast in the oven for 40 minutes until the flesh of the pumpkin is tender.

4. Remove from the oven and allow to cool a little. Roughly tear the mozzarella before scattering over the pumpkin along with the chopped nuts.

137

Mini vegetable quiches

SERVES: 4 | PREP TIME: 30 MINUTES | COOKING TIME: 35-40 MINUTES

INGREDIENTS

2 tbsp olive oil

1 small onion, finely chopped

1 large carrot, diced

1 courgette (zucchini), diced

3 large eggs

225 ml / 8 fl. oz / ¾ cup light cream

FOR THE PASTRY

100 g / 3 ½ oz / ½ cup low-fat butter, cubed

200 g / 7 oz / 1 ⅓ cups plain (all-purpose) flour

1 large egg, beaten

METHOD

1. To make the pastry, rub the butter into the flour until the mixture resembles fine breadcrumbs. Stir in enough cold water to bring the pastry together into a pliable dough and chill for 30 minutes.

2. Preheat the oven to 190°C (170° fan) / 375F / gas 5.

3. Roll out the pastry on a floured surface and use it to line 4 individual tart cases.

4. Prick the pastry with a fork, line with greaseproof baking paper and fill with baking beans or rice. Bake the cases for 10 minutes then remove the paper and baking beans.

5. Meanwhile, heat the oil in a frying pan and fry the onion, carrot and courgette for 5 minutes or until softened.

6. Gently whisk the eggs with the cream until smoothly combined then stir in the vegetables and season generously with salt and pepper.

7. Pour the filling into the pastry cases, then lower the oven temperature to 150°C (130° fan) / 300F / gas 2 and bake for 20 minutes or until just set in the centre.

Rice and pumpkin porridge

SERVES: 2 | PREP TIME: 30 MINUTES | COOKING TIME: 40 MINUTES

INGREDIENTS

50 g / 1 ¾ oz / ¼ cup brown rice

150 g / 5 ¼ oz pumpkin

100 ml / 3 ½ fl. oz / ½ cup almond milk

METHOD

1. Preheat the oven to 180°C (160°C fan) / 350F / gas 4. Soak the rice in cold water for 30 minutes.

2. Peel the pumpkin and roughly chop the flesh. Place onto a baking tray and roast in the oven for 20 minutes until softened.

3. Drain the rice and then cook as per the packet instructions.

4. Add the pumpkin to the rice along with the milk. Lightly blend together using a hand blender and gently heat to warm through.

5. Pour into a serving bowl and serve warm.

Fried cheese and onion sandwich

SERVES: 1 | PREP TIME: 5 MINUTES | COOKING TIME: 15 MINUTES

INGREDIENTS

1 tbsp olive oil

½ onion, sliced

1 tbsp Dijon mustard

2 slices of granary bread

50 g / 1 ¾ oz / ½ cup low-fat cheddar cheese, grated

METHOD

1. Heat the oil in a frying pan over a medium heat and fry the onion for 10 minutes until soft and translucent.

2. While the onions are cooking, spread the bread with the mustard.

3. Once cooked transfer the onions to one of the slices of bread and top with the grated cheese. Place the other slice of bread on top and place the sandwich into the frying pan. Squash down with a spatula and fry until browned, then flip over and cook the other side.

4. Serve immediately.

Fish bites with tartar sauce

SERVES: 2 | PREP TIME: 10 MINUTES | COOKING TIME: 15 MINUTES

INGREDIENTS

100 g / 3 ½ oz light mayonnaise

1 tbsp capers, chopped

2 gherkins, chopped

½ shallot, finely diced

1 lemon, juice

a handful of dill, finely chopped

a handful of flat leaf parsley, chopped

100 g / 3 ½ oz / ⅔ cup plain flour

1 tsp turmeric

a pinch of salt

150 ml / 3 ½ fl. oz sparkling water

250 g / 9 oz white fish (such as cod or pollock), cut into chunks

flour for dredging the fish

sunflower oil for frying

METHOD

1. Start by making the tartar sauce by mixing the mayonnaise with the capers, gherkins, shallot, lemon juice and herbs. Place in the fridge until required.

2. Combine the flour, turmeric and salt in a mixing bowl. Whisk together using a balloon whisk until smooth and no lumps are left.

3. Heat the oil in a deep fryer or in a wok to around 5 cm depth over a medium high heat, it will be hot enough when a drop of batter sizzles and crisps quickly when added to it. Dip the fish pieces into the flour and then the batter, allowing any excess to drip off. Place into the hot oil using a basket or slotted spoon and fry for around 5 minutes until golden. Remove and place onto kitchen paper to soak up any excess oil. Repeat until all the fish has been cooked.

4. Serve immediately with the tartar sauce and lemon wedges.

Mushroom and ricotta parcels

SERVES: 2 | PREP TIME: 10 MINUTES | COOKING TIME: 30 MINUTES

INGREDIENTS

2 tbsp olive oil

250 g / 9 oz Portobello mushrooms

2 garlic cloves, chopped

200 g / 7 oz spinach, washed

200 g / 7 oz low-fat ricotta cheese

3 sheets of filo pastry

1 tbsp butter, melted

½ leek, cut into thin strips

METHOD

1. Heat the oil in a large pan over a medium high heat. Cut the mushrooms into roughly 2 cm cubes and fry for 4 minutes until browned. Add the garlic and cook for 1 minute. Remove and set aside to cool.

2. Add the spinach and fry for 3 minutes until wilted. Remove onto kitchen paper, squeezing out as much liquid as possible. Roughly chop and add to the mushrooms.

3. Once cooled, mix the ricotta cheese into the mushrooms and spinach, seasoning to taste. Refrigerate until needed.

4. Preheat oven to 200°C (180°C fan) / 400F / gas 6. Cut the filo sheets into rough 20 cm (8 in) squares. Arrange three sheets on top of each other in a star shape brushing lightly with melted butter between each layer. Add a spoonful of the mushroom mixture in the centre of each star and bring up the edges to form a parcel. Tie the top using a thin strip of leek.

5. Place in the oven and bake for 15 minutes or until the pastry has turned golden brown.

Spicy lamb samosas

SERVES: 6 | **PREP TIME:** 20 MINUTES | **COOKING TIME:** 35 MINUTES

INGREDIENTS

2 tbsp olive oil

1 small onion, finely chopped

2 cloves of garlic, crushed

250 g / 9 oz / 1 cup minced lamb

¼ tsp chilli (chili) powder

½ tsp ground cumin

½ tsp ground coriander

¼ tsp ground cinnamon

50 g / 1 ¾ oz / ⅓ cup frozen peas, defrosted

225 g / 8 oz filo pastry

100 g / 3 ½ oz / ½ cup butter, melted

METHOD

1. Preheat the oven to 180°C (160° fan) / 350F / gas 4 and grease a large baking tray.

2. Heat the oil in a frying pan and fry the onion for 5 minutes or until softened.

3. Add the garlic and minced lamb and cook for 5 more minutes then add the spices and peas. Turn off the heat and leave to cool for a few minutes.

4. Cut the pile of filo sheets in half then take one halved sheet and brush it with melted butter.

5. Arrange a tablespoon of the filling at one end and fold the corner over, then triangle-fold it up.

6. Transfer the samosa to the baking tray and repeat with the rest of the filo and filling, then brush with any leftover butter.

7. Bake the samosas for 20 minutes, turning half way through, until the pastry is crisp and golden brown.

Pumpkin soup

SERVES: 4-6 | PREP TIME: 20 MINUTES | COOKING TIME: 40 MINUTES

INGREDIENTS

1 pumpkin

low calorie cooking spray

1 onion, diced

2 cloves of garlic, minced

1 tsp paprika

1 tsp cayenne

500 ml / 17 fl. oz / 2 cups low salt vegetable stock

METHOD

1. Preheat the oven to 180°C (160°C fan) / 350F / gas 4.

2. Peel the pumpkin and remove the seeds. Slice the flesh and place onto a baking tray before spraying over a little oil. Place into the oven and roast for 20 minutes until tender.

3. Place a large saucepan onto a medium high heat and spray with oil. Add the onion and cook stirring regularly for 5-6 minutes until softened. Add the garlic, paprika and cayenne and cook for a further minute.

4. Add the pumpkin and mix through the spices and onion. Add the stock and turn up the heat until boiling, cover and reduce to a simmer. Cook for 18-20 minutes before blending using a hand blender to make the soup smooth. Season to taste before serving.

Side salad with dressing

SERVES: 2-4 | PREP TIME: 10 MINUTES

●●●●●●●●●●●●●●●●●●●●●●●●●●●

INGREDIENTS

120 g / 4 ¼ oz crispy salad leaves

½ cucumber, sliced

4 large tomatoes, sliced

1 tbsp extra virgin olive oil

1 clove of garlic, minced

1 tsp white wine vinegar

1 tsp wholegrain mustard

METHOD

1. Wash the salad leaves and dry in a salad spinner.

2. Combine the leave with the cucumber and tomatoes in a large bowl.

3. Place the oil, garlic, vinegar and mustard into a sealable jar or container. Shake well to combine. Season with salt and black pepper to taste.

4. Pour the dressing over the salad and toss to coat the leaves when ready to serve.

Stuffed mushrooms

SERVES: 2-4 | PREP TIME: 10 MINUTES | COOKING TIME: 40 MINUTES

INGREDIENTS

low calorie cooking spray

1 shallot, diced

1 clove of garlic, diced

100 g / 3 ½ oz / ½ cup brown rice

200 ml / 7 fl. oz / ¾ cup water, boiling

a handful of parsley, chopped

6 Portobello mushrooms

100 g / 3 ½ oz / 1 cup lighter cheddar cheese, grated

METHOD

1. Preheat the oven to 180°C (160°C fan) / 350F / gas 4.

2. Spray the oil into a saucepan with a lid and place onto a medium high heat. Add the shallot and garlic and cook for 1-2 minutes. Add the rice, shallot and garlic for a minute.

3. Pour the water into the pan, it should bubble vigorously, before turning the heat down and covering. Leave to cook for 18-20 minutes until the rice has absorbed the liquid and is tender. Mix the parsley through the rice and season.

4. Place the mushrooms upside down onto a baking tray and remove the centre stalks. Spoon the rice into them and top with the grated cheese. Cook for 15 minutes, until the cheese has melted.

150

Egg fried rice with spinach

SERVES: 1 | PREP TIME: 10 MINUTES | COOKING TIME: 15 MINUTES

● ●

INGREDIENTS

1 egg, beaten

½ tsp sesame oil

½ tsp Chinese five spice

low calorie cooking spray

50 g / 1 ¾ oz / ¼ cup cooked brown rice, cooled

50 g / 1 ¾ oz spinach, washed

1 tbsp reduced salt soy sauce

METHOD

1. Place a non-stick pan onto a medium heat. Whisk the egg together with the sesame oil and five spice. Pour into the pan and cook to make an omelette, remove from the pan and set aside.

2. Spray the pan with cooking oil and add the rice. Cook for 8-10 minutes to heat through and the rice starts to crisp a little. Add the spinach and mix through the rice until it has wilted.

3. Roughly chop the omelette and return to the pan with the rice and fold through. Add the soy sauce and stir through the rice and egg.

4. Spoon into a bowl and serve immediately.

151

Courgetti with mushroom

SERVES: 2 | PREP TIME: 10 MINUTES | COOKING TIME: 10 MINUTES

INGREDIENTS

2 large courgettes (zucchini) or 300g
pre-made "courgetti"

200 g / 7 oz closed cup chestnut mushrooms, chopped

2 tsp olive oil

1 garlic clove, minced

25 g / 1 oz pomegranate seeds

METHOD

1. Using a spiraliser cut the courgettes into thin ribbons, known as courgetti. Alternatively cut lengthways into ribbons and then again into thin strips. Add to a pan of salted boiling water and cook for 2 minutes until tender, drain well and set aside.

2. Spray a frying pan with cooking oil and place over a medium heat. Sauté the mushrooms with the garlic until softened and the mushrooms have released their natural moisture.

3. Add the courgetti and stir through to heat before seasoning. Divide equally between two plates and garnish with pomegranate seeds and fresh basil.

152

Citrus and mozzarella salad

SERVES: 2 | PREP TIME: 15 MINUTES

INGREDIENTS

1 clementine

1 lighter mozzarella ball

1 tbsp olive oil

1 tsp chilli (chili) flakes

1 tsp honey

100 g / 3 ½ oz crispy leaf salad leaves

METHOD

1. Peel the clementine over a bowl and remove the segments, collecting any juice in the bowl. Set the segments aside.

2. Drain the cheese and slice into bite sized pieces.

3. Add the oil, chilli flakes and honey to the collected fruit juice and whisk. Season with salt and black pepper to taste.

4. Add the segments and cheese to the bowl with the dressing and toss to coat.

5. Divide the salad leaves between two serving bowls before spooning over the fruit and cheese with the dressing. Season with a little more salt and pepper before serving.

Chicken noodle soup

SERVES: 2 | PREP TIME: 15 MINUTES | COOKING TIME: 30 MINUTES

INGREDIENTS

2 chicken breasts

750 ml / 25 1/3 fl. oz / 3 cups low salt chicken stock

root ginger, peeled and sliced

1 lime

2 carrots, finely sliced

2 potatoes, peeled and diced

½ head of broccoli, florets only

75 g / 2 ½ oz. rice or wheat noodles

1 tbsp soy sauce

1 tbsp sesame oil

2 eggs, hard boiled

METHOD

1. Chop the chicken into bite sized pieces and add to a large saucepan with the stock, ginger and juice of the lime.

2. Place onto a high heat until boiling before covering and cooking until the chicken is tender, around 10 minutes.

3. Add the carrots, potatoes, broccoli and noodles to the soup and cook for a further 20 minutes until the vegetables are soft and noodles cooked.

4. Stir the soy sauce and sesame oil through the soup. Serve with the hard-boiled eggs placed on top, if desired.

Roast aubergine

SERVES: 1 | PREP TIME: 10 MINUTES | COOKING TIME: 25 MINUTES

INGREDIENTS

1 aubergine (eggplant)

1 red pepper

1 tomato

a handful of mint

1 tsp dill, chopped

METHOD

1. Preheat the oven to 200°C (180°C fan) / 400F / gas 6 and then change the setting to grill.

2. Pierce the aubergine a few times with a sharp knife. Place the aubergine and red pepper into a baking tray and place under the grill. Cook for 20 minutes turning occasionally so that the skin has blackened and the flesh softened.

3. Remove from the oven and set the aubergine aside to cool. Carefully peel the skin from the pepper and then roughly chop, removing the stalk and seeds. Chop the tomato and mix with the pepper and herbs.

4. Cut open the aubergine and season. Place onto a place and spoon the pepper and tomato into the aubergine.

Mushroom tartlets

SERVES: 6 | PREP TIME: 30 MINUTES | COOKING TIME: 30 MINUTES

INGREDIENTS

300 g / 10 ½ oz light shortcrust pastry

low calorie cooking spray

3 shallots, sliced

1 clove of garlic, minced

175 g / 6 oz mushrooms, sliced

100 ml / 3 ½ fl. oz / ½ cup lighter double (heavy) cream

100 g / 3 ½ oz / 1 cup light cheddar cheese, grated

1 tbsp parsley, chopped

METHOD

1. Preheat the oven to 180°C (160°C fan) / 350F / gas 4 and grease 6 tartlet cases.

2. Roll out the pastry to roughly 3mm / 1/8 in thickness before cutting circles to fit inside the cases. Place into the cases and gently press into the corners, place into the refrigerator for 20 minutes to chill.

3. Cover the pastry with greaseproof paper and weigh down with baking beans. Bake for 12-15 minutes until light brown and crisp. Remove and set aside.

4. Spray a non-stick frying pan with oil and place onto a medium heat. Add the shallots and garlic and cook for 3-4 minutes until fragrant and starting to colour. Add the mushrooms to the pan and cook for a further 5 minutes, seasoning with salt and black pepper. Remove from the heat to cool.

5. Mix the cream and cheese together and season before mixing through the parsley.

6. Fill the pastry cases with the cream and mushrooms. Place into a baking tray and bake in the oven for a further 8-10 minutes until the cheese has melted and set.

Quiche stuffed peppers

SERVES: 1-2 | PREP TIME: 20 MINUTES | COOKING TIME: 40 MINUTES

INGREDIENTS

2 peppers

low calorie cooking spray

1 shallot diced

1 clove of garlic, minced

1 chicken breast, finely diced

½ tbsp plain (all-purpose) flour

3 eggs, beaten

75 ml / 2 ½ fl. oz / ⅓ cup skimmed milk

75 g / 2 ½ oz / ¾ cup low-fat Cheddar cheese, grated

basil leaves

METHOD

1. Preheat the oven to 180°C (160°C fan) / 350F / gas 4.

2. Cut the top off the peppers and scrape out the seeds and membrane. Cut the edible flesh from the tops into chunks and set aside.

3. Place a frying pan on a medium heat and spray with the cooking oil. Add the reserved pepper pieces, shallot and garlic and cook for 2-3 minutes until softened.

4. Add the chicken to the pan and continue to cook for a further 8-10 minutes until the chicken is cooked and firm to the touch. Remove from the heat and set aside.

5. Whisk together the flour, eggs and milk before folding through the cheese. Add the chicken mixture to this and fold through. Season with salt and black pepper and add a few chopped basil leaves.

6. Spoon the quiche mixture into the peppers and place into an ovenproof dish where they can be securely placed upright.

7. Bake in the oven for 30 minutes until the filling has set and the peppers are roasted and starting to colour. Remove and serve warm with a garnish of basil leaves.

Sweet potato wedges

SERVES: 4 | PREP TIME: 15 MINUTES | COOKING TIME: 45 MINUTES

INGREDIENTS

800 g / 1 lb 12 oz sweet potatoes, cut into wedges
with the skin left on

1 tsp smoked paprika

60 ml / 2 fl. oz / ¼ cup olive oil

METHOD

1. Wash then parboil the sweet potatoes in boiling salted water for 5 minutes, then drain well and leave to steam-dry for 2 minutes.

2. Meanwhile, put the oil in a large roasting tin in the oven and heat it to 200°C (180°C fan) / 400F / gas 6.

3. Mix the smoked paprika with ½ a teaspoon of salt and pepper, then sprinkle the mixture evenly over the sweet potatoes.

4. Carefully tip the wedges into the roasting tin and turn to coat in the oil.

5. Bake the wedges for 45 minutes, turning every 15 minutes, until golden brown on the outside and fluffy within. Sprinkle with a little more salt and serve immediately.

Chicken and spinach rolls

SERVES: 2 | PREP TIME: 10 MINUTES | COOKING TIME: 30 MINUTES

INGREDIENTS

low calorie cooking spray

1 chicken breast, diced

2 large crusty rolls

2 eggs, beaten

75 g / 2 ½ oz / 1 ¾ cups light Cheddar cheese, grated

50 g / 1 ¾ oz / ½ cup spinach

METHOD

1. Preheat the oven to 200°C (180°C fan) / 400F / gas 6. Place the chicken onto a baking tray and season with salt and black pepper. Spray with a little oil before transferring to the oven. Bake for 12-15 minutes until firm to the touch and slightly coloured.

2. Cut the rolls in half and remove the soft white bread from the inside. Whisk together the eggs and cheese and season. Place the spinach in a colander over the sink and pour over a kettle of boiling water.

3. Combine the cooked chicken, egg and spinach before spooning into the rolls. Place the rolls into the oven on a baking tray and cook for 15 minutes, or until the egg has set and started to colour. Remove and serve.

161

Omelette with raw pepper salad

SERVES: 1 | PREP TIME: 10 MINUTES | COOKING TIME: 10 MINUTES

INGREDIENTS

low calorie cooking spray

1 shallot, diced

½ courgette (zucchini), diced

50 g / 1 ¾ oz spinach, washed

4 free-range eggs, beaten

50 g / 1 ¾ oz / ½ cup light cheddar cheese, grated

½ red pepper, sliced

½ yellow pepper, sliced

METHOD

1. In a non-stick frying pan heat the oil over a medium heat. Once hot, add the shallots and courgette and fry for 5 minutes stirring regularly. Add the spinach and cook for a further minute until wilted.

2. Pour the eggs into the pan and mix in with the vegetables so that they are equally distributed and the egg covers the pan. Season with salt and black pepper.

3. Cook for 5 minutes until the egg is cooked through and the bottom is crisp. Sprinkle over the grated cheese before folding over the omelette. Transfer to a plate and top with the raw peppers and season.

Griddled chicken wraps

SERVES: 2 | PREP TIME: 10 MINUTES | COOKING TIME: 20 MINUTES

INGREDIENTS

2 chicken breasts, trimmed

1 tsp cumin

1 tsp coriander (cilantro)

1 tsp paprika

½ lemon, juiced

low calorie cooking spray

2 tbsp reduced fat mayonnaise

1 yellow pepper, deseeded and sliced

½ red onion, sliced

¼ cucumber, sliced

2 tomatoes, sliced

50 g / 1 ¾ oz / ½ cup rocket (arugula)

2 tortilla wraps

METHOD

1. Slice the chicken breasts into two or three fillets, depending on their size. Mix them with the cumin, coriander, paprika, salt and pepper and lemon juice.

2. Place a griddle pan onto a medium high heat and once hot spray with the cooking oil. Place the chicken onto the griddle and cook for 12-15 minutes until firm to the touch and cooked through.

3. Place the mayonnaise, pepper, onion, cucumber, tomatoes and rocket into the centre of a wrap. Place the chicken on top and fold over, seal with a skewer or similar. lace the wraps back onto the griddle and toast for a few minutes before serving.

163

Potato wedges

SERVES: 4 | PREP TIME: 15 MINUTES | COOKING TIME: 45 MINUTES

INGREDIENTS

800 g / 1 lb 12 oz potatoes, peeled and
cut into wedges

1 tsp garlic powder

60 ml / 2 fl. oz / ¼ cup olive oil

METHOD

1. Parboil the potatoes in boiling salted water
   for 5 minutes, then drain well and leave to
   steam dry for 2 minutes.

2. Meanwhile, put the oil in a large roasting tin
   in the oven and heat it to 200°C (180°C fan) /
   400F / gas 6.

3. Mix the garlic powder with ½ teaspoon of
   salt and pepper, then sprinkle the mixture
   evenly over the potatoes. Carefully tip the
   wedges into the roasting tin and turn to coat
   in the oil.

4. Bake the wedges for 45 minutes, turning
   every 15 minutes, until golden brown on the
   outside and fluffy within. Sprinkle with a
   little more salt and serve immediately.

Braised spring vegetables

SERVES: 4 | PREP TIME: 5 MINUTES | COOKING TIME: 25 MINUTES

INGREDIENTS

2 tbsp olive oil

4 baby artichokes, halved

175 ml / 6 fl. oz / ⅔ cup dry white wine

2 leeks, cut into large chunks

8 shallots, peeled

12 small chantenay carrots, scrubbed

500 ml / 17 ½ fl. oz / 2 cups good quality vegetable stock

12 asparagus spears, trimmed

150 g / 5 ½ oz / 1 cup fresh peas

1 tbsp lemon juice

2 tbsp flat leaf parsley, finely chopped

METHOD

1. Heat the oil in a large cast iron casserole dish and sear the cut sides of the artichokes until well browned.

2. Pour in the wine and bring to the boil, then add the leeks, shallots, carrots and stock and bring back to the boil.

3. Reduce the heat and simmer gently for 10 minutes, then add the asparagus and peas and simmer for a further 8 minutes.

4. Add a squeeze of lemon then season to taste with salt and pepper and sprinkle with parsley.

165

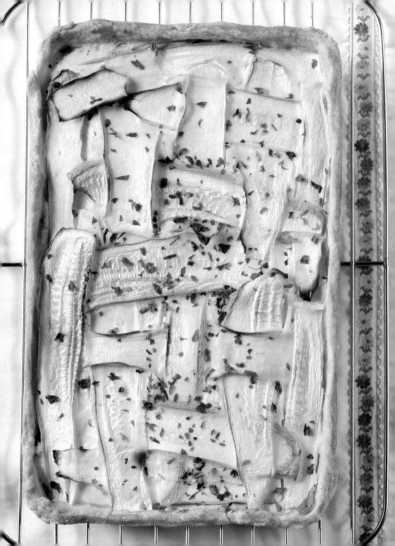

Courgette tart

SERVES: 4-6 | PREP TIME: 20 MINUTES | COOKING TIME: 45 MINUTES

INGREDIENTS

200 g / 7 oz light shortcrust pastry

low calorie cooking spray

1 onion, diced

1 clove of garlic, minced

1 tsp dill, chopped

1 tbsp low-fat butter spread

1 tbsp plain (all-purpose) flour

400 ml / 14 fl. oz / 1 ¾ cups skimmed milk

150 g / 5 ¼ oz / 1 ½ cups lighter
Cheddar cheese, grated

3 courgette (zucchini), sliced into ribbons

1 tbsp thyme leaves

METHOD

1. Preheat the oven to 180°C (160°C fan) / 350F /
   gas 4 and lightly grease a rectangular
   ovenproof dish.

2. Roll out the pastry to roughly 3mm thickness so
   that it is large enough to fill the dish. Place into
   the dish and gently push into the corners. Place
   into the refrigerator until required.

3. Spray a medium sized saucepan with oil and
   place onto a medium heat. Add the onions and
   cook for 5-6 minutes until softened. Add the
   garlic and dill and cook for a further minute
   until fragrant.

4. Add the butter spread to the pan and stir
   through until melted. Add the flour and
   mix into the onions, stirring to cook the
   flour for 2-3 minutes.

5. Pour the milk into the pan stirring at all times to
   avoid any lumps. Once added keep stirring until
   the sauce thickens. Once thickened add the
   cheese and mix through until melted and
   season with salt and black pepper.

6. Pour the sauce into the pastry case and even out
   with a spatula. Top with the ribbons of courgette
   before scattering over the thyme leaves.

7. Bake in the oven for 30 minutes so that the
   pastry has become crisp and the courgettes are
   cooked and browning at the edges.

Warm potato and vegetable salad

SERVES: 2-4 | PREP TIME: 15 MINUTES | COOKING TIME: 30 MINUTES

INGREDIENTS

250 g / 9 oz new potatoes

2 courgette (zucchini), chopped

2 tbsp low-fat butter spread

flat leaf parsley, chopped

100 g / 3 ½ oz tomatoes, chopped

METHOD

1. Place the potatoes into a pan of salted boiling water and cook for 20-25 minutes until softened. Drain and set aside.

2. Place the courgettes into a pan of boiling water and cook for 12-15 minutes until tender. Drain and set aside.

3. Place the potatoes and courgettes into a bowl and add the spread and parsley. Toss to coat with the spread and season with salt and black pepper.

4. Add the tomatoes and stir through the salad before serving.

Beef tacos

SERVES: 2 | PREP TIME: 10 MINUTES | COOKING TIME: 15 MINUTES

INGREDIENTS

1 tsp paprika

1 tsp cumin

1 tsp coriander (cilantro)

1 tsp chilli (chili) powder

200 g / 7 oz lean beef steak, sliced

low calorie cooking spray

1 onion, sliced

1 red pepper, deseeded and sliced

50 g / 1 ¾ oz / ½ cup sweetcorn

4 tomatoes, chopped

½ red onion, finely diced

1 lime, juiced

4 small corn tortillas

a handful of fresh coriander (cilantro), chopped

METHOD

1. Preheat the oven to 180°C (160°C fan) / 350F / gas 4.

2. Combine the spices with the meat in a bowl and toss to coat, set aside until needed.

3. Heat the oil in a non-stick frying pan over a medium high heat. Add the onions and peppers and fry for 6-8 minutes until soft and translucent.

4. Add the beef to the pan and mix through the onions, browning the meat as you stir. Add a splash of water to the pan to prevent the spices burning. Add the sweetcorn to the pan and continue to cook for 8-10 minutes until the beef is cooked.

5. Combine the tomatoes, red onion and lime juice in a bowl and season to taste.

6. Turn a muffin tin upside down and place the tortillas into the gaps to form a taco shape. Place into the oven and cook for around 5 minutes until crisp and holding their shape.

7. Serve the beef inside the taco shells with the tomato salsa on the side and fresh coriander.

Glazed carrots

SERVES: 2 | PREP TIME: 10 MINUTES | COOKING TIME: 20 MINUTES

INGREDIENTS

300 g / 10 ½ oz carrots

1 clove of garlic, minced

1 tbsp olive oil

1 orange, zested

1 tbsp fruit syrup

50 g / 1 ¾ oz / ½ cup walnuts, chopped

METHOD

1. Preheat the oven to 180°C (160°C fan) / 350F / gas 4.

2. Wash the carrots and scrape the surface with a sharp knife to peel.

3. Place the carrots into a bowl and toss together with the garlic, oil, orange zest and fruit syrup. Season with salt and black pepper.

4. Place onto a baking tray and roast in the oven for 20 minutes, removing a couple times to move the carrots around in the glaze.

5. Remove from the oven and place into a serving dish and scatter over the nuts.

Sliced baked potatoes

SERVES: 2-4 | PREP TIME: 15 MINUTES | COOKING TIME: 30 MINUTES

INGREDIENTS

4 large potatoes

2 cloves of garlic, minced

2 tbsp low-fat butter spread

1 tbsp olive oil

2 tbsp parsley, finely chopped

METHOD

1. Preheat the oven to 200°C (180°C fan) / 400F / gas 6.

2. Peel the potatoes and then thinly slice using a mandoline or sharp knife. Place into a bowl and set aside until needed.

3. Mix the garlic and butter spread together and grease an ovenproof dish with this mixture.

4. Place the sliced potatoes into the dish, arranging them in an attractive fashion with the slices all next to each other. Drizzle over the oil and season with salt and black pepper.

5. Transfer to the oven and roast for 30 minutes or until the potatoes have started to crisp and are tender.

6. Remove from the oven and scatter over the chopped parsley before serving.

Vegetable ragout

SERVES: 2 | PREP TIME: 15 MINUTES | COOKING TIME: 45 MINUTES

INGREDIENTS

low calorie cooking spray

1 onion, diced

1 clove of garlic, chopped

2 carrots, sliced

2 sticks of celery, sliced

2 potatoes, peeled and cubed

½ head of cauliflower, florets only

1 tbsp tomato purée

400 g / 14 oz chopped tomatoes

400 ml / 14 fl. oz / 1 ¾ cups low salt vegetable stock

50 g / 1 ¾ oz / ⅓ cup garden peas

fresh basil leaves, chopped

METHOD

1. Place a casserole pan onto a medium heat and spray with cooking oil.

2. Add the onions and cook for 5-6 minutes until softened. Add the garlic, carrots and celery and cook for a further 4-5 minutes.

3. Add the potato and cauliflower to the pan before adding the tomato purée. Mix through the vegetables to coat.

4. Add the chopped tomatoes and stock to the pan. Increase the heat until boiling before covering and reducing to a simmer. Cook covered for 30 minutes, adding the peas after 15 minutes, until the vegetables have softened.

5. Season the ragout with salt and black pepper to taste before stirring through the basil and serving.

Potato salad

SERVES: 4-6 | PREP TIME: 15 MINUTES | COOKING TIME: 20 MINUTES

INGREDIENTS

500 g / 1 lb baby potatoes, peeled and cubed

250 g / 8 ½ lbs / 1 cup low-fat greek yogurt

30 ml / 1 fl. oz extra virgin olive oil

1 tbsp capers

100 g / 3 ½ oz / ½ cup spring onions (scallions), finely sliced

a handful of fresh dill, finely chopped

METHOD

1. Place the potatoes into a pan of boiling salted water and cook for 15-20 minutes until just soft. Drain and set aside to cool.

2. Once cool combine the potatoes with the yogurt in a large bowl. Mix through the remaining ingredients and season to taste.

3. Serve as a side dish, ideal with cold meats or at a barbecue.

Onion rings

SERVES: 2 | PREP TIME: 1 HOUR | COOKING TIME: 15 MINUTES

INGREDIENTS

2 onions, sliced into 1 cm thick rounds

400 ml / 13 ½ fl. oz low-fat buttermilk

140 g / 5 oz / 1 cup plain flour

½ tsp cayenne pepper

300 ml / 10 fl. oz groundnut oil

50 g / 1 ¾ oz corn flour

180 ml / 6 fl. oz sparkling water

METHOD

1. Place the sliced onions into a baking dish and cover with the buttermilk. Cover with cling film and leave for up to an hour.

2. Put 100 g of the plain flour onto a plate with the cayenne and season. Drain the onions and coat them in the seasoned flour.

3. Heat the oil in a saucepan or fryer to 180°C / 350F. Meanwhile, make the batter by combining the remaining flour with the water and a pinch of salt until smooth.

4. Dip each onion ring into the batter and fry in the oil for 3-4 minutes until crisp. Remove when browned and place onto kitchen paper to dry and toss with salt.

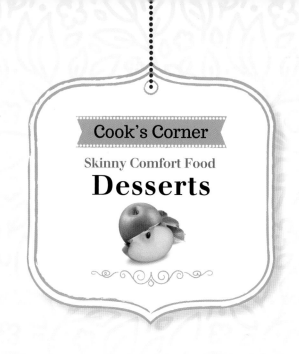

Cook's Corner

Skinny Comfort Food
Desserts

Vanilla cheesecake

MAKES: 1 | PREP TIME: 30 MINUTES | CHILLING TIME: 4 HOURS

••••••••••••••••••••••••••••

INGREDIENTS

FOR THE BASE

100 g / 3 ½ oz / ¾ cup pecans

200 g / 7 oz Medjool dates

100 g / 3 ½ oz almond butter

FOR THE FILLING

600 g / 1 lb 3 oz light cream cheese

100 g / 3 ½ oz / 1 cup icing sugar

2 vanilla pods, seeds only

300 ml / 10 fl. oz low-fat crème fraîche

dark chocolate sauce, to serve

METHOD

1. Place four 8 cm (3 in) pastry rings onto greaseproof paper on a baking tray.

2. In a food processor, blend together the pecans, dates and almond butter. Press into a large cheesecake ring and place in the fridge while you make the filling.

3. Mix the cream cheese, icing sugar and vanilla seeds in a mixer at a medium speed. Gradually add the crème fraiche until combined.

4. Spoon onto the cheesecake base and even out with a spatula. Refrigerate for at least 4 hours or overnight to set.

5. Remove from the fridge about 30 minutes before serving to come up to room temperature.

6. To remove the mould, place on top of a can and gently pull down the mould (heat the mould slightly, if necessary).

7. After slicing the cheesecake into wedges, drizzle with dark chocolate sauce to serve. Delicious served with fresh berries.

Trifle pots

MAKES: 6 | PREP TIME: 35 MINUTES | COOKING TIME: 10 MINUTES

INGREDIENTS

300 g / 10 ½ oz raspberry Swiss roll, sliced

100 g / 3 ½ oz / ⅔ cup strawberries, sliced

100 g / 3 ½ oz / ⅔ cup blueberries

100 g / 3 ½ oz / ⅔ cup raspberries

4 tbsp sherry

300 ml / 10 ½ fl. oz / 1 ¼ cups light cream

FOR THE CUSTARD

450 ml / 12 ½ fl. oz / 1 ¾ cups skimmed milk

1 vanilla pod, split lengthways

4 large egg yolks

75 g / 2 ½ oz / ⅓ cup caster (superfine) sugar

1 tsp cornflour (cornstarch)

METHOD

1. Layer the Swizz roll and fruit inside 6 glasses and drizzle over the sherry.

2. Combine the milk and vanilla pod in a saucepan and bring to simmering point.

3. Meanwhile, whisk the egg yolks with the caster sugar and cornflour until thick.

4. Gradually incorporate the hot milk, whisking all the time, then scrape the mixture back into the saucepan.

5. Stir the custard over a low heat until it thickens then spoon it into the glasses.

6. Leave the custard to cool to room temperature then whip the cream until it forms soft peaks and spoon it on top of the trifles.

Pumpkin cupcakes

SERVES: 12 | PREP TIME: 20 MINUTES | COOKING TIME: 50 MINUTES

INGREDIENTS

150 g / 5 oz pumpkin, sliced

150 g / 5 oz / 1 cup plain flour

1 tsp cinnamon

½ tsp ground ginger

½ tsp ground allspice

1 tbsp baking powder

1 tsp bicarbonate soda

100 g / 3 ½ oz / ½ cup low-fat butter

2 tbsp manuka honey

2 eggs

100 ml / 3 ½ fl. oz skimmed milk

150 g / 5 oz low-fat cream cheese

150 g icing sugar

1 tsp vanilla extract

pumpkin seeds

METHOD

1. Preheat oven to 200°C (180°C fan) / 400F / gas 6 and place the sliced pumpkin into the oven for 20 minutes until soft. Remove and when cooled remove the flesh and blend into a puree in a food processor or blender.

2. Place 12 muffin cases into a muffin tin, or lightly grease a muffin tin. Combine the flour, spices, baking powder and bicarbonate of soda in a large mixing bowl.

3. In a separate bowl, combine half the butter and manuka honey. Add the eggs, one at a time, and mix. Stir in the milk and pumpkin puree using a wooden spoon, followed by the flour mixture.

4. Spoon the mixture into the muffin cases and bake for 30 minutes until light and bouncy. Cool in the tin before removing to a wire rack.

5. Combine the cream cheese and remaining butter and beat until smooth. Gradually add the icing sugar then vanilla extract and mix until light.

6. Ice the cakes once cooled and sprinkle over some pumpkin seeds.

Banana, pear and chocolate pots

SERVES: 6 | PREP TIME: 5 MINUTES | COOKING TIME: 5 MINUTES

INGREDIENTS

200 ml / 7 fl. oz / ¾ cup light cream

200 g / 7 oz dark chocolate
(min. 60% cocoa solids, chopped

3 bananas, sliced

2 pears, cored and diced

100 g / 3 ½ oz amaretti biscuits, crushed

METHOD

1. Heat the cream until it starts to simmer, then pour it over the chopped chocolate and stir until the mixture has cooled and thickened.

2. Layer the chocolate ganache with the banana and pear inside 6 glass mugs and top with a sprinkle of crushed amaretti biscuits.

Pear and plum tarte Tatin

SERVES: 8 | PREP TIME: 10 MINUTES | COOKING TIME: 25 MINUTES

INGREDIENTS

3 tbsp low-fat butter, softened and cubed

2 tbsp manuka honey

4 pears, peeled, cored and quartered

12 small plums, stoned

6 mirabelles, stoned

250 g / 9 oz light puff pastry

METHOD

1. Preheat the oven to 220°C (200° fan) / 425F / gas 7.

2. Dot the butter and manuka honey over the base of a large ovenproof frying pan.

3. Arrange the pears round the outside of the pan, followed by a ring of plums and the mirabelles in the centre.

4. Roll out the pastry on a floured surface and cut out a circle the same size as the frying pan.

5. Lay the pastry over the fruit and tuck in the edges, then transfer the pan to the oven and bake for 25 minutes or until the pastry is golden brown and cooked through.

6. Using oven gloves, put a large plate on top of the frying pan and turn them both over in one smooth movement to unmould the tart.

Summer fruit and mint crumbles

SERVES: 6 | PREP TIME: 15 MINUTES | COOKING TIME: 25 MINUTES

INGREDIENTS

200 g / 7 oz / 1 ⅓ cups raspberries

200 g / 7 oz / 1 ⅓ cups blueberries

4 tbsp caster (superfine) sugar

3 sprigs of mint

75 g / 2 ½ oz / ⅓ cup low-fat butter

50 g / 1 ¾ oz / ⅓ cup plain (all-purpose) flour

25 g / 1 oz / ¼ cup ground almonds

METHOD

1. Preheat the oven to 180°C (160° fan) / 350F / gas 4.

2. Put the raspberries, blueberries, caster sugar and mint in a saucepan and cover it with a lid.

3. Heat gently for 5 minutes to soften the fruit and infuse it with mint, then discard the mint and divide the fruit between six individual baking dishes.

4. Rub the butter into the flour and stir in the ground almonds.

5. Crumble the mixture over the fruit then bake for 25 minutes or until the topping is golden brown.

Almond cake

SERVES: 8 | PREP TIME: 20 MINUTES | COOKING TIME: 1 HOUR

INGREDIENTS

200 g / 7 oz / ¾ cup low-fat butter

100 g / 7 oz / ¾ cup xylitol
(or alternative low-calorie sweetener)

4 eggs

150 g / 5 oz / 1 ½ cups ground almonds

50 g / 1 ¾ oz / ⅓ cup plain flour

1 tsp almond extract

icing sugar for dusting

METHOD

1. Preheat the oven to 180°C (160°C fan) / 350F / gas 4 and grease and line a 20 cm (8 in) cake tin. Cream the butter and xylitol until light and fluffy. Gradually beat in the eggs, one at a time, before folding in the almonds, flour and almond extract.

2. Pour the mixture into the prepared cake tin and even out with a spatula. Bake in the centre of an oven for 1 hour, or until a skewer inserted into the centre of the cake comes out clean. Remove to a wire rack to cool. Dust with icing sugar when ready to serve.

Pear frangipane tarts

SERVES: 8 | PREP TIME: 30 MINUTES | COOKING TIME: 2 HOURS

INGREDIENTS

2 ripe pears

2 tbsp honey

2 lemons, juice and zest

100 ml / 3 ½ fl. oz water

1 cinnamon stick

FOR THE BASE

200 g / 7 oz / 1 ⅓ cups plain flour

100 g / 3 ½ oz / ½ cup low-fat butter

1 egg

FOR THE FILLING

75 g / 2 ½ oz / ⅓ cup low-fat butter

75 g / 2 ½ oz / ⅓ cup caster sugar

2 eggs, beaten

75 / 2 ½ oz / ¾ cup ground almonds

1 tsp vanilla extract

METHOD

1. Preheat the oven to 190°C (170°C fan) / 375F / gas 5. Cut the bottom off the pears and stand in an oven proof dish. Mix the honey, lemon juice and water and pour over the pears, add the cinnamon. Bake for an hour basting with the syrup every 15 minutes. They should be slightly soft when ready, remove to cool.

2. Lightly grease a 28 cm loose bottomed fluted tart tin. Add the flour and butter into a food processor and pulse until it resembles breadcrumbs. Add the egg and a drop of water mixing until the dough forms.

3. Roll out the pastry on a floured surface as thinly as possible and place into the tart tin. Prick with a fork and set aside.

4. Make the frangipane by whisking the sugar and butter until creamy. Mix in the eggs, followed by the ground almonds and vanilla extract. Spoon into the tart base. Slice the pears and arrange on top.

5. Place on a baking tray and bake for 50 minutes until the pastry is crisp and tart is golden brown.

Raspberry upside down cake

SERVES: 6 | PREP TIME: 15 MINUTES | COOKING TIME: 25 MINUTES

INGREDIENTS

100 g / 3 ½ oz / ⅔ cup self-raising flour

1 tsp baking powder

100 g / 3 ½ oz / ½ cup caster
(superfine) sugar

100 g / 3 ½ oz / ½ cup low-fat butter, softened

2 large eggs

250 g / 9 oz / 2 cups fresh raspberries

icing (confectioner's) sugar for dusting

METHOD

1. Preheat the oven to 180°C (160° fan) / 350F / gas 4 and butter a 20 cm round cake tin.

2. Sieve the flour and baking powder into a mixing bowl and add sugar, butter and eggs.

3. Beat the mixture with an electric whisk for 4 minutes or until smooth and well whipped.

4. Arrange half of the raspberries in the cake tin and spoon the cake mixture on top.

5. Level the cake mixture with a palette knife and bake for 25 minutes or until a skewer inserted comes out clean.

6. Leave the cake to cool for 20 minutes before turning out onto a serving plate.

7. Top with the rest of the raspberries and sprinkle with icing sugar just before serving.

Lemon meringue pie

SERVES: 8-10 | PREP TIME: 45 MINUTES | COOKING TIME: 15 MINUTES

INGREDIENTS

FOR THE BASE

100 g / 3 ½ oz / 1 cup ground almonds

1 egg, whisked

1 tbsp plain flour

¼ tsp stevia

FOR THE CURD

3 eggs

100 g / 3 ½ oz / ⅓ cup honey

1 lemon, juice and zest

80 g / 3 oz / ⅓ cup unsalted, low-fat butter

FOR THE MERINGUE

4 egg whites

¼ tsp cream of tartar

100 g / 3 ½ oz / ½ cup caster sugar

METHOD

1. Preheat the oven to 200°C (180°C fan) / 400F / gas 6. Lightly grease a medium sized pie dish.

2. In a bowl, mix the almonds and egg, gradually adding the flour to form a non-sticky dough. Roll out and place into the pie dish, pushing into the corners and trimming off excess. Bake for 10 minutes until crisp.

3. For the curd, whisk the eggs and honey in a saucepan adding the lemon zest. Lower the heat and whisk until thickened and pale yellow. Add the lemon juice and butter, a little at a time, whisking until just starting to bubble. Pass through a sieve and set aside.

4. For the meringue, whisk the egg whites and tartar in a stand mixer on high until soft peaks form. Turn down the whisk and gradually add the sugar until thick and glossy.

5. Assemble the cake by spreading the cooled curd over the base and topping with the meringue. Place under a grill for 5 minutes or until the meringue has started to brown in places.

Fruits of the forest crumble

SERVES: 6 | PREP TIME: 10 MINUTES | COOKING TIME: 40 MINUTES

INGREDIENTS

450 g / 1 lb / 3 cups mixed forest fruits
(defrosted if frozen)

3 tbsp manuka honey

75 g / 2 ½ oz / ⅓ cup low-fat butter

50 g / 1 ¾ oz / ⅓ cup plain (all-purpose) flour

25 g / 1 oz / ¼ cup ground almonds

METHOD

1. Preheat the oven to 180°C (160° fan) / 350F / gas 4.

2. Mix the forest fruits with the manuka honey and arrange in an even layer in the bottom of a baking dish.

3. Rub the butter into the flour and stir in the ground almonds.

4. Squeeze a handful of the mixture into a clump and then crumble it over the fruit. Use up the rest of the topping in the same way, then shake the dish to level the top.

5. Bake the crumble for 40 minutes or until the topping is brown and the fruit is hot and bubbling.

Muffins with chia seeds

SERVES: 12 | PREP TIME: 10 MINUTES | COOKING TIME: 25 MINUTES

INGREDIENTS

3 lemon, zest and juice

4 tbsp xylitol

300 g self raising flour

2 tbsp chia seeds

250 ml almond milk

60 g / 2 oz / ¼ cup low-fat butter, melted

2 large free range eggs, beaten

METHOD

1. Preheat the oven to 200°C (180°C fan) / 400F / gas 6 and lightly grease a muffin tin.

2. Combine the lemon zest and xylitol together and mix thoroughly. Add the flour and chia seeds and mix well.

3. In a separate bowl, whisk together the almond milk, butter, lemon juice and egg until light. Make a well in the centre of the dry ingredients and pour in the egg mixture. Stir just enough to combine, not any more, as this will affect the texture.

4. Spoon the mixture into the muffin tin in equal amounts and place into the oven for 20-25 minutes until a skewer inserted into the centre comes out clean.

5. Remove from the tin and allow to cool before serving.

Dairy-free almond butter cookies

MAKES: 12 | PREP TIME: 10 MINUTES | COOKING TIME: 15 MINUTES

INGREDIENTS

200 g / 7 oz almond butter

150 g / 5 oz / ¾ cup light brown sugar

1 egg

1 tsp vanilla extract

50 g / 1 ¾ oz / ½ cup ground almonds

sea salt for sprinkling

METHOD

1. Preheat the oven to 200°C (180°C fan) / 400F / gas 6 and line a baking tray with grease proof paper. In a bowl, mix together the almond butter, sugar, egg and vanilla extract. Once combined stir in the ground almonds until you have a stiff dough.

2. Using your hand roll pieces of the dough into a ball the size of a cherry tomato. Flatten and place onto the baking tray and sprinkle with sea salt.

3. Place into the oven and bake for 10 minutes until lightly golden. Remove to cool on the tray for 5 minutes and then a wire rack to cool completely.

Lime and vanilla stewed pineapple

SERVES: 6 | PREP TIME: 5 MINUTES | COOKING TIME: 10 MINUTES

INGREDIENTS

150 ml / 5 ½ fl. oz / ⅔ cup pineapple juice

1 lime, juiced and zest thinly pared

1 vanilla pod, split lengthways

1 pineapple, peeled, cored and cut into chunks

3 tbsp runny honey

coconut ice cream to serve

METHOD

1. Put all of the ingredients in a saucepan and bring to a gentle simmer.

2. Stew the pineapple for 10 minutes, then leave to cool completely.

3. Serve with scoops of coconut ice cream.

Nectarine and blackberry tart

SERVES: 8 | PREP TIME: 30 MINUTES | COOKING TIME: 45 MINUTES

INGREDIENTS

90 g / 3 oz / ½ cup sunflower spread

65 g / 2 ⅓ oz / ⅓ cup xylitol

3 free-range egg yolks

200 g / 7 oz / 1 ⅓ cups plain (all-purpose) flour

2 nectarines, ripe

150 g / 5 ¼ oz / 1 cup blackberries

2 tbsp honey

1 tsp cornflour (cornstarch)

100 g / 3 ½ oz reduced sugar apricot jam (jelly)

mint leaves to garnish

METHOD

1. Preheat the oven to 180°C (160°C fan) / 350F / gas 4 and lightly grease a fluted tart tin.

2. Cream together the sunflower spread and xylitol in a bowl before adding the egg yolks one at a time. Sift the flour into the bowl and bring together to form a ball of dough.

3. Turn out onto a lightly floured surface and knead until smooth. Wrap in cling film and place into the refrigerator for 20 minutes while you make the filling.

4. Half the nectarines and remove the stone. Slice the halves into smaller pieces and place in a bowl with the blackberries. Stir the honey and cornflour into the fruit and set aside.

5. Roll out the pastry between two sheets of greaseproof paper to roughly 3mm thickness. Place into the tart tin and push the pastry into the edges.

6. Cover the base of the tart with the apricot jam before arranging the fruit on top.

7. Bake in the oven for 40-45 minutes until the pastry is crisp and golden.

8. Remove and set aside to cool before garnishing with the mint leaves.

Crispy marshmallow squares

MAKES: 16 | PREP TIME: 2 HOURS, 10 MINUTES

COOKING TIME: 10 MINUTES

INGREDIENTS

2 tbsp coconut oil

1 tsp vanilla extract

250 g / 9 oz sugar free marshmallows

150 g / 5 oz puffed rice

100 g / 3 ½ oz dark chocolate
(min. 70% cocoa solids)

METHOD

1. Lightly grease a 22 x 33 cm (9 x 13 in) tin and set aside.

2. In a large saucepan, add the coconut oil and heat gently to melt, stirring in the vanilla extract. Add the marshmallows and gently melt then stirring all the time. Once melted add the puffed rice and completely mix into the marshmallow. Quickly transfer to the prepared tin ensuring that it is even and flat across the whole tin.

3. Leave to set for 2 hours before cutting into 16 cubes.

4. Before serving, melt the chocolate in a heatproof bowl over simmering water. Drizzle across the marshmallow cubes using a spoon.

Mini pear and quinoa crumbles

SERVES: 4 | PREP TIME: 15 MINUTES | COOKING TIME: 40 MINUTES

INGREDIENTS

200 g / 7 oz / 1 cup quinoa

1 cinnamon stick

4 pears, peeled and cubed

1 tbsp manuka honey

50 g / 1 ¾ oz / ¼ cup low-fat butter, melted

50 g / 1 ¾ oz / ½ cup ground almonds

75 g / 2 ½ oz / ½ cup dark brown sugar

METHOD

1. Preheat the oven to 200°C (180° fan) / 400F / gas 6.

2. Put the quinoa and cinnamon in a saucepan with 450 ml water and bring to the boil. Cover the pan, then reduce the heat and simmer gently for 15 minutes or until all the water has been absorbed.

3. Spread the quinoa out onto a tray and leave to steam dry for a few minutes.

4. Toss the pears with the manuka honey and divide them between four individual baking dishes.

5. Stir the melted butter, ground almonds and brown sugar into the quinoa, then sprinkle the mixture on top of the pears.

6. Bake the crumbles in the oven for 25 minutes or until the tops are golden brown.

Mango dessert

SERVES: 2 | PREP TIME: 10 MINUTES | COOKING TIME: 30 MINUTES

INGREDIENTS

1 mango, peeled and de-stoned

1 tsp fruit syrup

500 ml / 17 fl. oz low-fat Greek yogurt

fresh sliced strawberries, to garnish

METHOD

1. Place the mango into a food processor and blend to a purée.

2. Place two thirds of the yogurt into the bottom of two serving glasses before adding a layer of mango purée. Top with the remaining yogurt and chill for 30 minutes or until needed.

3. Before serving, top with the sliced strawberries.

Cranberry and oat muffins

MAKES: 12 | PREP TIME: 15 MINUTES | COOKING TIME: 20 MINUTES

INGREDIENTS

150 g / 5 oz / 1 ½ cups rolled oats

100 g / 3 ½ oz / ½ cup self-raising flour

1 tsp baking powder

1 tsp cinnamon

100 g / 3 ½ oz / ½ cup light muscovado sugar

100 g / 3 ½ oz / ⅔ cup cranberries

1 lemon, zest

200 ml / 6 ½ fl. oz skimmed milk

3 tbsp sunflower oil

1 egg, lightly beaten

METHOD

1. Preheat the oven to 180°C (160°C fan) / 350F / gas 4 and line a 12 hole tin with muffin cases. Place the oats into a blender and grind to a fine powder. Combine with the flour, baking powder, cinnamon, sugar, cranberries and lemon and mix.

2. In a separate bowl, mix the milk, oil and egg. Make a well in the centre of the dry ingredients and gradually pour in the milk and egg mixture. Mix just enough to combine the ingredients, no more, and spoon into the muffin cases. Bake in the oven for 20 minutes until risen and firm to touch.

Creamy apple and honey dessert

SERVES: 4 | PREP TIME: 10 MINUTES

INGREDIENTS

200 g / 7 oz low-fat crème fraiche

150 g / 5 oz 0% fat greek yogurt

50 g / 1 ¾ oz / ¼ cup honey

2 meringue shells, crushed

1 apple, cored and sliced

1 tbsp bee pollen

METHOD

1. In a bowl, fold together the crème fraiche, yogurt and honey.

2. Add the crushed meringue and mix through.

3. Spoon the mixture into serving glasses and top with apple slices and a small amount of bee pollen.

Small summer berry crumbles

SERVES: 6 | PREP TIME: 10 MINUTES | COOKING TIME: 25 MINUTES

INGREDIENTS

200 g / 7 oz / 1 ⅓ cups raspberries

200 g / 7 oz / 1 ⅓ cups strawberries, halved

2 tbsp manuka honey

75 g / 2 ½ oz / ⅓ cup low-fat butter

50 g / 1 ¾ oz / ⅓ cup plain (all-purpose) flour

25 g / 1 oz / ¼ cup ground almonds

40 g / 1 ½ oz / ¼ cup light brown sugar

METHOD

1. Preheat the oven to 180°C (160° fan) / 350F / gas 4.

2. Mix the raspberries and strawberries with the manuka honey and divide them between six ramekin dishes.

3. Rub the butter into the flour and stir in the ground almonds and brown sugar.

4. Crumble the mixture over the fruit then bake for 25 minutes or until the topping is golden brown.

Heart-shaped brownies

SERVES: 9 | PREP TIME: 30 MINUTES | COOKING TIME: 1 HOUR, 30 MINUTES

INGREDIENTS

125 g / 4 ½ oz reduced-fat sunflower spread

2 free-range eggs

125 g / 4 ½ oz light soft brown sugar

75 g / 2 ¾ oz self-raising flour

50 g / 1 ¾ oz cocoa powder, sieved, plus extra
to decorate

50 g / 1 ¾ oz plain dark chocolate, chopped

1 tsp chocolate extract

METHOD

1. Preheat the oven to 190°C (170° fan) / gas 5.
    Grease and line a large square deep cake
    tin or oven dish.

2. Beat together the sunflower spread, eggs and
    sugar. Stir in the flour and cocoa powder and
    add the chocolate and chocolate extract.
    Mix in 1 teaspoon of boiling water and
    a pinch of salt.

3. Transfer the mixture to the tin and bake for
    30 minutes, or until a skewer comes out clean
    when inserted in the centre.

4. Leave to cool in the tin then cut into hearts
    with a heart-shaped cutter. Dust with icing
    sugar. Top with a raspberry each, if desired.

Chocolate orange mousse

SERVES: 4 | PREP TIME: 20 MINUTES | CHILLING TIME: 4 HOURS

INGREDIENTS

100 g / 3 ½ oz dark chocolate, 80% cocoa solids

1 tsp Cointreau

1 tbsp cocoa powder

1 orange, zest only

2 egg whites

1 tbsp sugar

50 g / 1 ¾ oz low-fat yogurt

METHOD

1. Place a heat proof bowl of a pan of simmering water taking care it does not touch the water. Break up the chocolate and gently melt in the bowl adding the Cointreau, cocoa powder and 1 teaspoon of the orange zest. Remove from the heat as soon as it has melted and set aside.

2. Whisk the egg whites in a mixer until soft peaks form. Gradually add the sugar whilst continuing to whisk until it becomes thick and glossy.

3. Mix together the cooled melted chocolate with the yogurt until combined. Gently fold in a tablespoon of the egg using a metal spoon, before folding in the remaining egg without knocking out the air.

4. Spoon into serving glasses and chill for at least 4 hours or overnight.

5. Top with the remaining orange zest before serving.

Apple tea cake

SERVES: 6-8 | PREP TIME: 15 MINUTES | COOKING TIME: 45 MINUTES

INGREDIENTS

200 g / 7 oz / ¾ cup light butter spread

200 g / 7oz / ¾ cup xylitol

4 eggs

150 g / 5 ¼ oz / 1 ½ cups ground almonds

50 g / 1 ¾ oz / ⅓ cup plain (all-purpose) flour

2 apples, peeled and cored

METHOD

1. Preheat the oven to 180°C (160°C fan) / 350F / gas 4 and grease and line a loaf tin.

2. Cream the butter spread and sugar until light and fluffy. Gradually beat in the eggs, one at a time, before folding in the almonds and flour

3. Chop the apples into bite sized cubes and mix half through the batter.

4. Pour the mixture into the prepared cake tin and even out with a spatula. Top the cake with the remaining chopped apples.

5. Bake in the centre of an oven for 45 minutes, or until a skewer inserted into the centre of the cake comes out clean.

6. Remove from the oven and place on a wire rack to cool.

Poached pear and almond tart

SERVES: 4-6 | PREP TIME: 20 MINUTES | COOKING TIME: 1 HOUR, 45 MINUTES

INGREDIENTS

2 ripe pears

2 tbsp honey

2 lemons, juice and zest

100 ml / 3 ½ fl. oz / ½ cup water

1 cinnamon stick

100 g / 3 ½ oz / ½ cup low-fat butter spread

100 g / 3 ½ oz / ½ cup xylitol

2 eggs, beaten

100 g / 3 ½ oz / 1 cup ground almonds

1 tsp vanilla extract

50 g / 1 ¾ oz / 2/3 cup flaked (slivered) almonds

METHOD

1. Preheat the oven to 190°C (170°C fan) / 375F / gas 5 and lightly grease a 23cm square cake tin.

2. Cut the bottom off the pears and stand in an oven proof dish. Mix the honey, lemon juice and water and pour over the pears, add the cinnamon. Bake for an hour basting with the syrup every 15 minutes. They should be slightly soft when ready, remove to cool.

3. Whisk together the butter and sugar until pale and creamy. Stir the eggs into the butter mixture before folding in the ground almonds and vanilla extract.

4. Pour the cake mixture into the pan. Slice the pears into halves and place into the corners of the cake tin. Sprinkle the top with the flaked almonds.

5. Place into the hot oven and bake for 45 minutes until the top of the cake is golden brown and a skewer inserted into the cake comes out clean. Remove to cool before serving.

INDEX